MW01147898

Eric's Heart...
When a Mother Grieves

LAURA LYNN SARGENT

lauralynnsargent.com

WESTBOW
P R E S S®
A DIVISION OF THOMAS NELSON
& ZONDERVAN

Copyright © 2015 Laura Lynn Sargent.

All rights reserved. No part of this book may be used or reproduced by
any means, graphic, electronic, or mechanical, including photocopying,
recording, taping or by any information storage retrieval system
without the written permission of the publisher except in the case
of brief quotations embodied in critical articles and reviews.

*This book is a work of non-fiction. Unless otherwise noted, the author
and the publisher make no explicit guarantees as to the accuracy of
the information contained in this book and in some cases, names of
people and places have been altered to protect their privacy.*

Scripture taken from the Holy Bible, NEW INTERNATIONAL VERSION®.
Copyright © 1973, 1978, 1984 by Biblica, Inc. All rights reserved worldwide.
Used by permission. NEW INTERNATIONAL VERSION® and NIV® are
registered trademarks of Biblica, Inc. Use of either trademark for the offering
of goods or services requires the prior written consent of Biblica US, Inc.

WestBow Press books may be ordered through booksellers or by contacting:

WestBow Press
A Division of Thomas Nelson & Zondervan
1663 Liberty Drive
Bloomington, IN 47403
www.westbowpress.com
1 (866) 928-1240

Because of the dynamic nature of the Internet, any web addresses or
links contained in this book may have changed since publication and
may no longer be valid. The views expressed in this work are solely those
of the author and do not necessarily reflect the views of the publisher,
and the publisher hereby disclaims any responsibility for them.

Any people depicted in stock imagery provided by Thinkstock are
models, and such images are being used for illustrative purposes only.
Certain stock imagery © Thinkstock.

ISBN: 978-1-4908-8340-3 (sc)
ISBN: 978-1-4908-8341-0 (e)

Library of Congress Control Number: 2015909049

Print information available on the last page.

WestBow Press rev. date: 06/23/2015

Contents

This book is dedicated to my mom, Laura, Eric's Grammy

You are so much a part of this book. You're every page, every word; you were by my side in the happy times and the saddest of times. You have been a godly example my entire life; I can't begin to count the times I've thanked God for you. And I continue to thank Him...

Foreword

In Eric's Heart, Laura Lynn Sargent gently takes us by the hand and lets us accompany her through moments of joy, anxiety, raw edginess, desperation, uncertainty, hope, sorrow, grief, and finally triumph. The walk begins with something every parent fears: the newborn baby is born unexpectedly with something terribly wrong--- with Eric, it was severe heart disease.

Lynn's story, Eric's story, crashes into our quiet and routine lives, jolts us with jumbled emotions, and guides us to places where we sometimes would rather not be. And to places we all long for. During the journey we find Lynn discovering gentle power and strength alongside her indomitable sense of humor.

Eric's story is ultimately one of love, joy, and peace. For me, it is more than an accounting of the ups and downs of my little red headed friend with an impish grin. Much more. Any sadness in his short life is erased by a profound sense of gentleness and joy, of triumph over tragedy, and of grace over grief. Lynn reassures us that Eric's very being did not end with the last beat of his heart, but that he happily lives on still in a place he had once visited.

Thank you, Lynn, for sharing Eric's life with us, and for bringing him back for a visit!

John H. Gay, MD

Preface

Eric was my dream come true, my firstborn, my baby boy! He was born on Mother's Day, May 8, 1977. Every new mom's life changes after her baby is born and I was no different. Well, thankfully, my experience was different than most. The changes Eric's life made to mine transformed me forever...

Eric was born with severe congenital heart disease. He survived four heart surgeries, the first at only 42 hours and the last three within 11 months. He never felt sorry for himself. Eric taught me so many things about life, that life is fragile, but yet, should be lived with joy, love and reckless devotion to those closest to us.

As you get to know Eric through my memories, I hope you will laugh and cry along with me as I recall his silly side, his strong unbending faith in God and the strength of a child facing multiple medical giants. You will also be amazed at God's gentle continual care of Eric, as I am amazed, and through Eric, my faith is now steadfast.

After Eric died, I longed to read Christian books by other mothers who had lost a child. I only found one. I needed encouragement... encouragement to get up in the morning... encouragement to turn to God with my sorrow. I needed to know there was hope for my shattered heart; the long dark nights and the rude awakening every morning to my first thought: yes, my son had really died and I had another day to face. God was faithfully ministering to me, but I needed to hear from another mother that what I felt, maybe she felt too.

It's been over 30 years since Eric died, and now it's my turn to offer encouragement: your broken heart will heal, and in time, you will live again. I cling to the assurance that Eric is in Heaven. My Heavenly Father promises life is eternal through belief in His Son, Jesus. I also know, without a doubt, that God can't lie. He is Truth. Jesus says in *John 14:6, "I am the Way, the Truth and the Life. No one comes to the Father except through Me."*

As time moves on, I'm closer to seeing my precious red headed son again. This time it's forever, there will be no good-byes!

Acknowledgements

Steve

You are the love of my life... you've told me you don't know where you end and I begin; and I don't know where I end and you begin. Our love is eternal! You never knew Eric, but as I've shared memories of him, you feel as though you had. As you read this book, your tears for me came from a heart woven together with my own. You share my faith and you believed in me as I began this journey of writing Eric's story. I love you for that. I love you for just being you!

Con Githens, my Dad

Thank you for all of the time you sacrificed so that Mom could be with Eric and me. I'm sure you went through several jars of peanut butter! Most importantly, thank you for being a godly dad to me; your example of living out your faith every day has given me a foundation that has withstood the test of time.

Jordan

I see your tender heart in so many ways; it's God's handprints on your soul. You have stepped into Eric's role as Lindsie's big brother; he passed the baton to you. I saw it when you catered her wedding. You protected her by making sure that her vegetarian entrée was purely vegetarian – no ingredient containing a hidden animal product made it past you. You even assumed Eric's role of bickering with Lindsie back in the day and I considered it quite healthy!

Lindsie

I wish Eric could see you now: a wife and a mother. You do it well, better than anyone I know. Usually it's the daughter asking the mother for advice, with us; it's the other way around! You lost so much on that day in January 1984. As God healed your broken heart, He molded you into the beautiful woman you are today and I am so proud of you, so thankful to be your mom.

Brody

I hope that the words on these pages will paint a picture for you so that the mystery of your brother, Eric, will no longer be that – a mystery. Like you, he loved music. Had he lived, the two of you would have filled the house with piano and strings and harmony! However, there's still time... we'll have eternity and as I sit here and imagine it... I am crying tears of joy!

Dr. John Gay

Dr. Gay, time and time again, I thought of how blessed we were that you were Eric's doctor. I don't believe it was out of happenstance, it was definitely God's design. You came into our lives when Eric was only 28 hours old and you were there to his last breath. You are most brilliant, and yet, most humble and your quiet faith in God resonates – sometimes without words - to those of us who are fortunate enough to have witnessed it. You made our difficult days a little more bearable. And now, you've made the writing of this book even more meaningful as God blessed us with the privilege of reconnecting after 30 years!

Annie, Beth, Gwen, Jana, and Kathy
My dearest friends, you are treasures. I love our long talks, knowing anything shared, is received with a surplus of grace and acceptance! Thank you for reading Eric's story and your words of encouragement that chased away much of my fear of taking it to the next step!

Eric

I cried tears of joy when I found out I was going to have a baby! It was the fall of 1976 and I had just turned 21. At the time, 21 seemed so old – I had married when I was 18 in December of 1973 - my girlfriends were having babies and I wanted to be a mommy too!

I grew up in Adel, a small Iowa town, 20 miles from Des Moines, the state's capital. My dad was a high school teacher and coach. We've always known Dad taught school so he could coach basketball, baseball, cross-country and golf. Luckily for him, I had a brother because I wasn't all that interested in sports. My mom was a stay-at-home mom, there was never a time that my mom was too busy or distracted to sit and talk with me about whatever was on my mind. My parents are enjoying retirement now and I'm happy for them.

My pregnancy was amazingly easy – no morning sickness – no scares or concerns. I was blessed with months of sweet little baby kicks and stretches and hiccups! I wrapped my arms around my round tummy and gave my little one lots of hugs.

My due date was May 6th, which was also my grandmother's birthday. Had Eric arrived on Grandma's birthday, we all would have been thrilled. If not, I at least hoped to be a mother by Mother's Day, and that's what happened! It was a gorgeous spring morning and I'd planned to spend the day honoring my mom and grandmas. When the first few labor pains began, I called my doctor. He didn't think it was a good idea for me to drive 20 miles away from the hospital; not to mention eating a big Mother's Day meal. So off to the hospital it was.

Mother's Day

After ten hours of labor, Eric was born at 10:05 p.m., May 8, 1977 – my first Mother's Day. He was perfect – 7 pounds 12 ½ ounces and 19 inches long. He was perfectly formed too – ten fingers and toes and a beautiful face and best of all – he had my strawberry blonde hair! The perfect end to a beautiful spring day.

Since it was late, I decided to wait until morning to make all of my calls to friends and family. This was back when there were no cell phones to text 50 people at once or internet with social media! One of my grandmothers had waited and waited to hear from me. She lay awake the whole night worrying that I was still in labor. She had given birth to five kids and the last two were twins – in a sense she labored along with me - unfortunately for her, it lasted ALL night! I felt terrible for not calling her, even at midnight.

First Sign of Trouble

After lying in my post-partum room all night and breathing in the sweet realization that I had a precious baby boy to snuggle and tenderly kiss morning, noon and night... a nurse from the nursery came with the first stroke of sad news. Eric was having trouble maintaining a normal body temperature. Also, his color, rather than a healthy newborn pink, was dusky and his lips, fingers and toes were cyanotic (blue). Cyanosis occurs when the blood is starved for oxygen and we were soon to find out that Eric's blood was severely starved for oxygen. Eric was placed in an isolette, which is an enclosed chamber with regulated temperature and oxygen. The nurse encouraged me to come to the nursery as much as I wanted to see Eric. She also said specialists were being called in to examine him. Little did I know that that very day the mature 21 year old that I thought I was, was about to truly grow up.

My faith in my God was about to be challenged; the first of many walks through the Refiner's fire. I am blessed that I was raised in a solid Christian family. My parents are strong Believers and we were active in church throughout my upbringing. Of course, it was a natural reaction for me to turn to the many prayer warriors in my life. This was the first time I'd known the power of intercessory prayer. Through the prayers, I had a constant underlying awareness of God's presence and He gave me strength to trust Him with my sweet son's life.

Laura Lynn Sargent

So many things have changed in 30 years. Post-partum rooms usually had two moms in them. I felt sorry for my roommate because I likely put a damper on her cherished time with her newborn baby. I tried so hard to be upbeat for her, but whenever the nurse brought my roommate's baby into our room – I turned to the wall and buried my face in my pillow trying to muffle my sobs. I so badly wanted to have Eric there in my arms too.

The first specialist to see Eric was a pediatrician who ran a gamut of tests on him including an EKG that came back normal. None of the tests revealed an abnormality. Late that afternoon the doctor returned and conveyed that he believed Eric was simply struggling to adapt to his new environment. He recommended keeping him in the isolette for another day or two and afterward he should be fine. The news was a relief because all of my joy had seemed to vanish with the nurse's 6:00 a.m. visit that day.

When my post-partum nurse asked if I'd like a sleeping pill at bedtime, I said yes. I had a fun day ahead getting back to snuggling my baby boy and I needed a good night's sleep! Well the happiness was short lived. Eric continued to struggle and the pediatrician was called in again later that night. After examining Eric, the doctor came to my room and said something was indeed wrong with Eric, he suspected his heart, but was unable to determine conclusively if it was his heart.

Even though Eric's EKG was normal, the pediatrician decided to call in a pediatric cardiologist, Dr. John Gay.

Once again I awakened to specialists who'd come to see Eric. Dr. Gay said Eric had symptoms of congenital heart disease, but to be certain it would require more tests. However, he'd wait until morning to see if Eric showed any signs of improvement. I told Dr. Gay that I had faith in God and would pray earnestly for my baby.

All through my pregnancy, I never once had a thought that my baby could have an internal defect. I worried about external defects: missing or deformed limbs or a disfigured face – but something internal, something deadly never once crossed my mind. Again, that was the 21 year old me who'd never encountered a critical illness or the death of anyone close.

The next morning I decided to visit Eric in the nursery. Before I got to the nursery door, I saw through the window a small crowd of white coats and stethoscopes around my tiny son. Fearing what I might hear, I turned around and went back to my room. I knew I was about to receive another visit from Dr. Gay and I feared I wasn't going to like what he had to say. Sure enough, Dr. Gay said Eric needed more tests and he needed to be transferred to Mercy Hospital about a mile away. The usual hospital stay for moms and newborns back then was three days. So that meant Eric went to Mercy Hospital and I stayed at Lutheran Hospital where he was born. However, a few hours later I was released and on my way to be with my son. Rather than leaving the hospital joyfully with my baby in my arms, I left with empty arms and tears streaming down my face.

Eric's heart...

Eric was only 42 hours old when he had his first heart surgery. Prior to surgery, he underwent a heart catheterization. Halfway through the procedure, Dr. Gay discovered that Eric's heart was missing the pulmonary artery. The pulmonary artery carries blue blood (or unoxygenated blood) from the right ventricle to the lungs. Before birth, babies receive their nutrition and oxygen from their mother through the umbilical cord. Thus, there is a lesser need for blood to flow to the lungs. While in the womb, a small blood vessel called the ductus arteriosus channels blood between the pulmonary artery and the aorta. (The aorta supplies oxygenated blood to the body.) After birth, the ductus arteriosus gradually closes as the baby breathes and the heart and lungs begin their lifelong partnership. All of this to say that the procedure was halted when Dr. Gay discovered Eric was missing his pulmonary artery; it was a race against the ductus arteriosus, before it completely closed. The procedure performed on Eric was the Blalock Tausig Shunt. The shunt compensates for the lack of a pulmonary artery by using the subclavian artery to reroute or shunt blood to the lungs. The Blalock Tausig Shunt is a palliative operation that gives heart babies time to grow and gain strength before a more invasive, and hopefully final, surgery.

I got to Mercy Hospital about the time Eric was out of surgery. I wasn't even 48 hours post-partum. I have to say I was quite smashing walking around the hospital carrying my "donut." My trophy! Of course when I wasn't carrying it, I was sitting on it.

After surgery, Eric was taken to the Surgical Intensive Care Unit. The place is mostly filled with adult patients so the little ones are extra special. I found my sweet baby lying in a tiny bed, hooked up to noisy machines monitoring heart rate, rhythms, body temps and the respirator supporting every effort he made to breathe. I looked down at my Eric and thought, oh you must love your mommy to fight so hard to live and oh how your mommy loves you.

I reluctantly left the hospital later that evening so that I could go home and rest. Sleep definitely didn't come easily. Thoughts of what should have been filled my mind along with thoughts of my tiny son fighting for his life. My prayers were continual and I asked God to awaken me in the night if Eric needed prayer, and trusting that He would, sleep finally came.

When I got to the hospital the next morning a few tubes were missing from that little fighter of mine. Dr. Gay appeared optimistic and the nurse asked me if I wanted to hold Eric?! Are you serious? I said a few tubes were missing, but many more were still attached. But hold my baby? I sat in a chair next to his bed, and I held my breath as she gently gathered tubes and bottles and my newborn son and placed him in my aching arms. Even now I write this with joyful tears as I recall how my own heart nearly burst. Oh how I loved this babe. Thank you, Jesus.

After only two weeks in the hospital, Eric came home. What a happy day! I was thankful that my God had answered my prayers and the prayers of so many who kept us lifted up. At the same time, I was worried that Eric was so fragile that a slight mistake would send us right back to the hospital. My fears were for naught. Eric was right on target with weight gain and all of his motor skills. The only giveaways that he was a heart baby were his blue fingertips and lips – unfortunately, the shunt didn't change that.

Severe Congenital Heart Disease

When Eric was ten months old, Dr. Gay said it was time to complete the heart cath started at birth. Because outwardly Eric looked like a healthy ten month old, Dr. Gay expected to have good news for us.

I don't think anyone gets used to seeing a little person being wheeled along a hospital corridor; especially the babies because their beds look more like cages than cribs. Saying good-bye outside the cath lab and seeing the fear in Eric's eyes as he looked at the strangers carrying him away was almost more than I could handle. If only I could take his place, if not, then let me feel all of the physical pain for him.

The heart cath seemed to last an eternity. As Dr. Gay finally walked toward us, I studied his face. I didn't know him well yet, but I sensed a somber air. I braced myself as Dr. Gay began to deliver the news as gently as possible. He used to say all too often, "I don't want to be pessimistic, but I have to be realistic."

My sweet Eric was a very sick little boy. His heart had several critical defects, all operable, but one. For starters, he was diagnosed with Tetralogy of Fallot. Patients with Tetralogy of Fallot have four various defects, that together, leave the body starved for oxygen. He also had a condition called endocardial cushion defect. This happens when the walls separating all four chambers of the heart are poorly formed or absent and the heart becomes one large chamber. We knew at birth that Eric had pulmonary atresia and the Blalock Tausig Shunt was performed to shunt blood to the lungs for oxygen. It was discovered that the aorta, which is the artery that carries oxygenated blood to the body, was attached to his right (only) ventricle; Dr. Gay called this defect in Eric D-transposition of the great vessels. Normally this defect is called transposition of the great vessels; it's when the pulmonary artery originates from the left ventricle and the aorta the right ventricle. A simpler way to say it is when the aorta and pulmonary artery are crisscrossed or switched. Eric had no left ventricle and no pulmonary artery, when his aorta originated in his only ventricle, in a sense, it corrected itself even though it was still backward.

After several attempts to view the left side of Eric's heart, Dr. Gay arrived at the conclusion that there was no left side to his heart. Eric's heart had only 2 ½ chambers; a normal heart has four. This was the inoperable defect. To the best of my knowledge, to this day, no correction has been perfected to correct or compensate for missing chambers. Without four chambers, Eric's heart wouldn't be strong enough to support an adult body. What it all came down to was Eric had a life expectancy of 17 to 18 years.

While we conferred with Dr. Gay, Eric was wheeled to his room on the pediatrics floor. When I got there, a nurse was rocking him. He was crying hysterically and I asked if I could take him. Eric was bleeding heavily at the sight where the catheter had been inserted. The nurse wanted to hold him and apply pressure to get the bleeding stopped. After several minutes, she was needed elsewhere on the floor so reluctantly she gave my baby boy to me along with instructions on how to hold him. As soon as he was in my arms, he snuggled closely and relaxed. As his body quieted, the bleeding stopped.

I grieved for my son two separate times: upon his death and six years earlier when I was told nothing could be done to correct his heart disease. We left the hospital the day after his heart cath. To add one more layer of pain to an unbearable load, Eric had stomach and intestinal flu. I was already grieving for my son, wasn't that enough? Anytime our children get sick whether it's flu, strep throat, ear infections – we moms can't relax for even a moment until they're well again. It's so hard to watch them suffer.

As I tried to find my way through this dark time, I spent a lot of time praying and searching for a ray of hope. I knew God could heal Eric. I've heard many testimonies of healing and so many people prayed, along with me, for his healing. That's how I coped. Dr. Gay said we had 18 years and I believed either God would make Eric whole or medical advances would find the way. I couldn't accept anything else, especially death.

I was blessed to attend a strong church where the congregation truly came along side us. I not only had Christian fellowship, I learned more about God through His Word. I met girlfriends through weekly Bible studies and another group of women with whom I taught Sunday School. I have to confess as to why I taught Sunday School... I wish my reason were noble or righteous. The truth is, I had trouble getting out of bed Sunday mornings so I needed a commitment! It turned out, though, to be a sweet blessing because I loved the children and my new girlfriends. Also, many years later, my daughter, Lindsie, married the son of one of my Sunday School teacher friends!

Memories of Eric

Over the next several years, life was normal for Eric. He grew in size and spirit. He liked Sesame Street, Scooby Doo, Star Wars and Lawrence Welk! He watched Lawrence Welk with his great grandparents – not me! Eric was not restricted from anything because of his heart disease. He rode his big wheel, learned to swim and liked rides at amusement parks – just to mention a few. Occasionally, Eric was short of breath following physical activities. However, he stopped napping altogether by the time he was three! Mommy was not quite ready for that!

When Eric was four years old his baby sister, Lindsie, was born. A week before Lindsie arrived I thought I might be going into labor and so went to the hospital for what turned out to be a false run. I had only been away a couple hours and when I got home, Eric ran full speed to the car excitedly asking "mommy do you have the baby?" It made me stop to think how quickly the new baby would be here and how different it would be for Eric and me. So on that hot July afternoon Eric and I went to Adventureland Amusement Park – what a sight I was with a swollen tummy and swollen feet! I had trouble keeping track of Eric... once I turned a full circle before I found him – he had been hidden under my belly!

First Glimpse of Baby Sister

Eric & Grammy Peeking at Lindsie

Ornery Eric Holding Lindsie

Even though Eric and Lindsie only had 2 ½ years together, I have a lifetime of memories tucked in my heart. I remember one evening not long after Lindsie's birth feeling an overwhelming sense of fulfillment unlike ever in my life. I had my son and my daughter both sleeping peacefully and contentedly. I wanted this season to last forever. Many times in my life I've looked forward to something special, but when that something finally gets here, I'm disappointed. The anticipation was far greater than the real thing... except when it came to my babies. After nine long months of pregnancy, becoming a mommy was all that I dreamed it would be and more!

When the first baby is born, everything changes. Life wraps itself around this precious gift from God. The second baby simply falls into the rhythm already in motion. Of course, I'm her mom, but I have never known a sweeter baby than Lindsie. She blended into our family's everyday life with ease. Even to this day Lindsie lives the beauty God talks of in 1 Peter 3:3&4: "Your beauty should not come from outward adornment, such as braided hair and the wearing of gold jewelry or fine clothes. Rather, it should be that of your inner self, the unfading beauty of a gentle and quiet spirit, which is of great worth in God's sight." God just made Lindsie that way, and I have always been envious. I ask God to grow in me a gentle and quiet spirit that He loves, we're still working on it.

Eric and Lindsie had very different temperaments. Lindsie, as I've described, was gentle and quiet. Eric was not. He made friends easily and knew no strangers... including the mom nursing her baby at the local kiddy pool. She was modestly draped, but Eric figured out what she was doing. I should have seen the wheels turning... next thing I heard was Eric asking the mom, "Is that chocolate milk?" I felt I needed to scold him, but found it nearly impossible while I was trying to hold back my own laughter. On another occasion a group of us went for pizza. The restaurant was packed and it was seat yourself or stand. By the time our group was able to get tables together, Eric had made friends with an older couple sitting close-by. They invited him to join them and they shared their pizza with him!

Eric loved his Grammy, my mom. I didn't realize he knew Grammy's phone number until the day I couldn't find Lindsie. I had a hunch and thankfully was right, within a few minutes, I found her at the park close to our house. What a scare! I told Eric not to tell Grammy because I didn't want her to know how irresponsible I'd been. However, I expected him to tell her and he did. He went straight into the house and called her before I could stop him!

Then there was the night Eric frightened me in a similar way. He went with me to pick-up a pizza; the restaurant was small and crowded. I had my back to him while I wrote a check for the pizza and when I turned around, he was gone! I looked in the back dining room, front dining room – no Eric. I was close to panicking and shouting for help when a woman brought him to me. She'd found him outside! My first reaction was to hug Eric and dismiss all of the thoughts of what could have happened to him and when I thought to thank the woman who'd found him, she was gone. I was so sorry that I hadn't immediately thanked her.

My mom laughs at the time she took Eric shopping. He sat in the cart while she shopped, Eric looked at his grammy, and in an endearing tone said, "Are you my fat little grammy..."

Grammy sang in a gospel group called the Kingdom Heirs. They stayed busy singing at various venues: churches, fairs, banquets, etc. Eric was their biggest fan. He sat enthralled every time he went to a concert and that was as often as possible. At home, he performed imaginary concerts with the Kingdom Heirs several times a day. He sang on a makeshift stage into anything that resembled a microphone. He pretended he was a Kingdom Heir and he usually sang a song by Dallas Holmes called "Hey! I'm a

Believer," and of course, the crowd gave standing ovations every time.

I remember one day giving Eric some cooked broccoli for lunch along with his favorite mac and cheese. Without even tasting the broccoli, he looked down and said, "Mommy, I can't like those trees."

We watched a Charlie Brown Christmas special one year and Eric kept looking for Charlie Brown's mommy. It troubled him that she wasn't in the story; he related it to himself and me. He was secure in knowing I was close. Eric brought so much joy to my life.

Eric attended preschool from the time he was three until he went to kindergarten. One year he sang a solo at the annual Christmas program! He sang "Come on Ring Those Bells"! After watching Grammy sing on stage with the Kingdom Heirs, there was no hesitation... he was living his dream!

Sometimes when Eric asked for something, I'd charge him two kisses and three hugs. He'd always give me four kisses and five hugs or more! So unlike his sister who'd only give one kiss, and no hugs and that was on a good day. Now when one of her girls won't hug or kiss her I tell her it's sweet revenge!

Fall 1982

In August of 1982, I wasn't prepared for a change in the tide. We went for Eric's regular six-month checkup with Dr. Gay. These six-month visits had become routine over the past five years and I fully expected the usual: "he's doing great, see you in six months." Dr. Gay had heard a faint murmur in Eric's heart six months earlier. He hoped it had dissipated, but sadly, he not only heard the murmur, it went from a grade two to a grade five in just six months; grade six being the worst. This meant we were hospital bound for Eric's third heart cath. Dr. Gay also said that the purpose of doing a heart cath is to make a surgical decision, the thought of surgery was terrifying.

In the time leading up to the heart cath, I had everyday life to contend with: clothes didn't wash themselves, and meals didn't simply appear on the table. I was restless, I couldn't sit still, but housework certainly didn't pacify me. Without realizing it, I was treating Eric differently, too. I tried to shelter him, but he overheard conversations. He perceived enough to know something was about to happen to him. When he misbehaved I didn't correct him, this left him confused, and it actually magnified his fear. Poor behavior escalated, and I continued to coddle him until I realized what I was doing... affirming his fears. I recognized that he needed the same consistent boundaries as always, he found security in that. He needed me to be strong for him. Eric's fears were soon replaced with courage; because we would face this together. If Mommy was strong, he was too.

The cath confirmed that Eric had a grade five leak in his aortic valve and it needed to be repaired. Remember, at ten months we were told nothing could be done to help Eric. However, cardiologists and cardiac surgeons are gaining ground all the time in the development of corrective procedures for congenital heart disease. Because of these successes, Dr. Gay was becoming hopeful that, with minor adjustments, we may have a ray of hope for Eric's heart. The corrections needed to be staged in two separate surgeries, six or more months apart. Since the leaky valve required immediate attention, it might be beneficial to begin corrective surgery at the same time as the valve repair rather than leaving the need for more surgeries later. A point of discussion was, realistically, how many times can a child safely undergo open heart surgery without succumbing to the stress of multi operations? Should we decide to wait, most likely Eric would eventually slip into heart failure, making his heart weak and unable to tolerate corrective surgery. The options were thoroughly discussed among the pediatric cardiologists, heart surgeons and our family. Of course, my family and I prayed earnestly for God's guidance and with a sense of peace we stepped forward in faith. We all agreed that with the valve necessitating surgery immediately, this was the time to begin the two-part correction.

God's People

We were sent home after the heart cath and before surgery. Once again, just like at Eric's birth, we asked for prayer. I am amazed at the power of prayer. When people are praying for you, you know it.

One particular Sunday evening, the church service was exceptionally powerful and the prayer time as well. A very godly, very humble man in my church asked if he could pray with Eric. I sat several rows away from them. After they finished, my friend came to me and said that he told Eric to imagine Jesus coming that very night to his bedroom and Jesus touching him.

Eric Met Jesus

Eric went right to bed when we got home from church; he seemed relaxed. The next morning he told me that Jesus had come to his room. He described Jesus as having a white robe with a "gold ribbon over his shoulder and across His chest." His eyes grew big as he described the sash, that it was brilliant, shiny. Eric had no doubt whatsoever that Jesus had come to him. I am not one who blindly jumps onto the wagon begging to hear more. I always approach cautiously, with a lot of doubt. My neighbors at the time were strong Believers and I shared with them what Eric had told me. My neighbor had had the very same experience when he was a child and the gold sash is what he remembered most about Christ's appearance.

Here's what I found in scripture:

> *Revelation 1:13:*
> *...and among the lampstands was someone "like a son of man," dressed in a robe reaching down to his feet and with a golden sash around his chest.*

Eric was only five and had never heard the Revelation 1:13 description of Jesus. Nor was I grounded in scripture and was unaware of Revelation 1:13 as well. It was very exciting later when I learned that the resurrected Jesus is dressed in a white robe with a brilliant gold sash.

The time leading up to Eric's surgery was tense. I worried about him catching a cold or flu bug that would cause surgery to be rescheduled. Another concern I had was for Lindsie. I was blessed to have most of my family in the Des Moines area. Thankfully, my grandparents offered to keep Lindsie and with big hearts of love and open arms for hugs. Having her there knowing she was doted on all day and night relieved me of any concerns for her. I always said that my grandma took better care of Lindsie than I did. She kept a journal when Lindsie stayed, it was fun to read and cute that Grandma even did it in the first place.

Preparing for Surgery

When Dr. Gay called to discuss a few details about Eric's surgery, he said he needed to conduct another heart cath before surgery to collect a little more information. He had mentioned after the previous cath that Eric had trouble relaxing and required additional anesthesia. We blamed it on Eric's fear and anxiety, mostly his fear of needles. His anxiety was reminiscent of the cath at ten months when he didn't relax until I held him. We had a little time to ponder a solution... what if I went into the cath lab while he was being prepped? Maybe he'd calm down easier and not resist the meds? Eric asked Dr. Gay, and after some thought, Dr. Gay agreed. I stayed with Eric until the anesthesia was administered and he was asleep. This was the first time he'd fallen asleep quickly and without an extra dose of sedation!

With the heart cath out of the way, it was time for surgery. I made the mistake of taking a tour of the Surgical Intensive Care Unit (SI) with Eric the night before his surgery. On our tour, we saw a patient, an older man, who was three hours post op. He was heavily sedated and on a respirator. I realize that a respirator is a lifesaving machine, but watching it breathe for someone who looks nearly dead is troubling. It's especially disturbing when your child will be lying there the next day. I was consumed in my own thoughts and trembling with fear when I almost didn't hear Eric ask if we could leave. His voice was barely audible and the color in his face was gone. The tour hadn't been such a good idea.

God provided comfort for us later that evening... I called a close friend of ours who had had open heart surgery several months earlier. I used a phone in a vacant room so that Eric couldn't hear my conversation with Jerry. I told Jerry about our tour of the Unit. Based on his own experience, he was able to share the encouragement we needed. He assured me that Eric wouldn't remember the surgery or the rest of the day in SI. Eric would be sedated and sleeping peacefully. I shared Jerry's assuring words with Eric, and he too, was comforted. Whenever fear tried to overtake me, God countered it by reminding me of Jerry's words. I never - never ever – would have chosen this road, but the intimacy with God was something I wouldn't have known any other way. As I lay in a small chair/sleeper next to Eric's bed that night, I prayed myself to sleep. I prayed of course for my precious little boy and I prayed fervently for the doctors who needed a restful night's sleep.

September 1982 Surgery

Grandparents arrived early the next morning and we all walked alongside our brave Eric babe as we made our way to the operating room. He rode to surgery in a little red wagon clutching a stuffed animal in each arm. I did my best to help Eric understand the reason for the surgeries, heart caths, needle pokes, etc. He always listened and trusted me and cooperated every time. This child of mine made me so proud.

On the Way to Surgery

We said good-bye to my son in the "holding" area as Eric was taken to the operating room. My last glimpse, was of him holding out his hands and crying for me. It nearly pulled the life right out of me. I walked down the hallway to the operating room (OR) waiting room, Eric's tears left me with an even greater heartache than I'd already had. What if something went sorely wrong that day and Eric didn't make it through surgery? That would have been my last memory of him.

Friends from church had said they'd come for the surgery, but I really didn't expect anyone. I was wrong. The room was packed with familiar faces. Some people took time away from work, others came after dropping off their kids at school. I had never in my life experienced such an outpouring of love and support. My mom just shook her head and said "your friends." I can't find words to express how much we were blessed – even 30 years later.

Eric was in surgery all morning. Thankfully OR nurses and Dr. Gay came to the waiting room periodically with progress reports. By lunchtime, Eric's surgery was finished and he was settled in SI and we were able to see him. The ultimate goal for the corrective surgery was to route blue blood to the lungs and red blood to the body. It sounds like it should be simple, but the body tends to rebel. When blood is rerouted, there is a change in the pressure of blood flowing to or from different areas of the body. Because of those changes, Eric's face was extremely puffy, that along with the respirator, he was barely recognizable. In fact, Eric's dad was so overcome at the sight of his son that his legs gave out from under him. Fortunately, Dr. Gay saw it coming and caught him before he hit the floor.

Unexpected Trauma

Pediatric cardiologists and heart surgeons were in Eric's room. The atmosphere was upbeat, as they conversed about the surgery, until one of the surgeons looked down at the drainage tube. The drainage tube is inserted directly below the chest incision. What should have been a mix of mostly clear fluid and a little blood, had become solid blood. In a matter of seconds the atmosphere shifted from "a job well done" air to a whirlwind of motion to get Eric back into surgery. It was lunchtime and most of the OR team had left the area. Urgent stat calls went out over the speaker system to summon the surgical team back to the OR. There had been no time for Dr. Gay to explain what was happening, but it obviously was imperative to get Eric back into the OR! I was left in a panic; I feared I was losing my son at that very moment and I melted to the floor and sobbed uncontrollably. My mom sat on the floor with me, put her arms around me and fervently prayed. Her heart was breaking too. She has always said that the sorrow was twofold for her: she hurt for me and she hurt for Eric. Not sure a heart can handle a load like that without God's strong arm.

Fortunately, the crisis was short lived with Eric soon settling back into his room in SI. An internal stitch on an artery had come loose; thankfully, the doctors were right there when it happened.

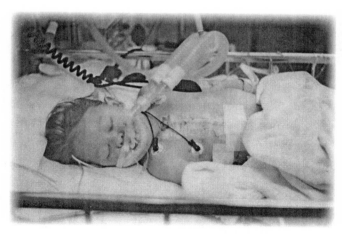

Post Op

Even with the trauma over, the surroundings were still overwhelming and intimidating. I don't think a mother could ever become callous to seeing her child, regardless of age, lying in a bed attached to multiple tubes and wires and monitors fighting to live. The respirator prohibited Eric from talking and all he could do was plead with his eyes for me to help him. It hurt to the core that I couldn't do anything, that's when I'd pray. Thankfully, he was "extubated" the next morning; that was the best news since surgery!

I was especially thankful for my mom. It was important to Eric and us that one of us stay with him all of the time. My mom selflessly took the night shift so that I could be at the hospital during the day to talk to the doctors. The rooms in SI aren't conducive to overnight family members so my mom sat in a chair all night next to Eric's bed. Mom would go home to sleep and then come back the next night to do it all again. Once Eric was moved to the peds floor I had a hide-a-bed and stayed around the clock. Because of my mom's sacrifices, Eric was never alone. Eric and I were blessed.

Postpericardiotomy Syndrome

Most heart kids stay in SI a couple days and most are released from the hospital before Eric was even moved back to the pediatrics floor. His recovery had been on track until he started running a temp and his heartbeat skyrocketed. His blood work didn't indicate an infection.

Eric always seemed to be a challenge for the docs and this time was no different. Postpericardiotomy Syndrome was the diagnosis. It sounded worse than it actually was. Postpericardiotomy Syndrome is an inflammation of the pericardium and pleural sac obviously a result of surgery. Another way to describe it is it's a combination of Pericarditis (sac around the heart) and pleurisy (sac around the lungs). Postpericardiotomy Syndrome is treated with prednisone initially and is then followed long-term by aspirin.

Challenged Myself to Learn about Eric's Heart

I had never attempted to learn about Eric's heart defects because I thought it was out of my reach. He had medical professionals who had years of education treating him. I was convinced that I could never grasp it so why try.

During our hospital stay I listened to several conversations about Eric. There seemed to be a lot of interest in Eric's heart. It became evident to me that his heart was unique, but not unique in a good way. I decided to make an effort to learn as much as I could about the heart. Dr. Gay gave me a copy of a letter he'd sent to Eric's pediatrician, which listed his congenital heart defects.

After we were released from the hospital, I went in pursuit of all the reading material I could find about the heart. The best resource was a book from the public library. The book explained the heart's anatomy and had a chapter that thoroughly covered congenital heart disease. Also, a friend who was a biology teacher, gave me a beautiful drawing of the heart that he'd drawn for one of his classes. The book, together with the drawing, enabled me to learn so much about the heart, and most importantly, Eric's heart. I was able to get my mind around what I thought was unattainable.

The more I read, the more I realized how severe Eric's heart defects were and the more I was amazed at his abilities in spite of his heart. Had I known, I might have been overly protective! I didn't restrict his physical activity – that was up to him. An interesting observation: a certain toy Eric and Lindsie each played with as babies. The toy was heavy for Eric to lift, but Lindsie swung it around as if it was as light as air.

Spring 1983

We took a family vacation a few weeks before Eric's April surgery to Galveston, Texas. Galveston was the closest shore and we were ready for water and warmth. The kids enjoyed gathering shells on the beach and staying in a hotel. On the way home, we stopped at a fast food restaurant with an outdoor play area. Eric found some children to play with, but apparently he felt a bit left out. So he thought that maybe he'd impress them by telling them, in detail, about his upcoming surgery. I heard tidbits of the conversation about the chest incision and respirator. Most children try to impress with tales of football, baseball or the latest toy, but a graphic description of heart surgery was a new one.

Occasionally Eric had a mild potty mouth. Never profane, yet it bordered more on the crude side. I'm quite certain it was all for my benefit, had I ignored it, the language would have faded away. Since it persisted, we needed a plan to cure his potty mouth... We decided the perfect opportunity was during his next surgery. As long as they were in there, the surgeons would surgically remove all of those "inappropriate" words. The amazing thing is I don't think we ever heard those words again! It must have worked!

The Most Intense Season

April came. Some days it seemed like it hit overnight and other times one day felt like 100 days. Either way life couldn't move on until this surgery was behind us. We spent a few days in the hospital leading up to the surgery for pre-op tests and checks. Even though I'd gained ground in my understanding of the heart, I wasn't prepared for the severity of this surgery.

The surgeons, anesthesiologists and pediatric cardiologists met with us in a conference room on the peds floor to revisit the risk of Eric's surgery. What had already been done the previous fall to Eric's heart was proving successful and that was an encouragement, but not a guarantee that the rest of the corrective procedure would succeed as well. This surgery entailed significantly more of what the prior surgery had begun. Without the surgery, Eric faced certain death and with it he was given a greater chance to live. Other children had undergone similar procedures and thrived. With much prayer and seeking God's will, we believed Eric would thrive too.

The weight of what lay ahead was sometimes lightened with visits and phone calls; I was thankful for the momentary breaks. One that stands out even now was the day Dr. Gay's wife, Jacki, brought lunch. Eric had a favorite sandwich shop across from the hospital – Millie's. We had asked if we could leave the hospital for a short trip to Millie's, but instead, Jacki brought sacks of tenderloins and fries.

Laura Lynn Sargent

Maybe not so healthy, but once in a while it was worth the joy it gave my sweet babe!

In the months prior to this surgery, I had developed a close friendship with a gal from church. Bambi's baby was born with serious congenital heart disease also. Thankfully, she's grown now, and for the most part, doing very well at overcoming what was a serious and persistent heart defect. Bambi and I will always have this bond. She called the day before Eric's surgery to tell me she believed God had given her scripture to share with me:

Psalm 116:1-5 (NIV)

I love the Lord, for he heard my voice;
he heard my cry for mercy.
Because he turned his ear to me,
I will call on him as long as I live.
The cords of death entangled me,
the anguish of the grave came over me;
I was overcome by distress and sorrow.
Then I called on the name of the Lord:
"Lord, save me!"
The Lord is gracious and righteous;
our God is full of compassion.

Up to that point I had trouble keeping myself composed. Once I start to cry, I'm a mess - I can't stop crying. The scripture Bambi shared helped me find the strength to face the day. I won't say it completely lifted my spirits, but it reminded me that God wanted to encourage me

32

to trust Him. Trusting God doesn't mean tragedy can't happen to Christians. We still face sorrow, and I was braced for that possibility. I knew God would see us through no matter what.

Just as the previous surgery, I didn't sleep well the night before. I prayed continually. Dr. Gay's phrase: "I don't want to be pessimistic, but I have to be realistic" best described my thoughts and concerns.

April 1983 Surgery

This time the walk to the OR was familiar. However, Eric had a different anesthesiologist who met us in the holding area. He administered the first dose of anesthesia to Eric as I held him. Rather than Eric crying for me as he was taken to surgery, this time he was barely awake and peaceful. What a difference.

I was met again in the OR waiting room by several family members and friends. So many amazing people so many conversations; they truly helped pass the time. And this surgery was grueling. The updates didn't come as often as before. Knowing the risk and complexity of this procedure, the waiting filled me with an almost unbearable sense of fear and anxiety. After nearly five hours, Dr. Gay came to give us a progress report. I expected him to say they were closing and we could see Eric shortly, but... they'd just gotten through the scar tissue from the last operation! They hadn't even started the actual procedure! He said that scar tissue has the consistency of cement and when cutting into flesh there's a risk of severing arteries – especially when, like in Eric's case, veins and arteries are in unusual places.

Surgery lasted another four hours... an eternity. We were thankful for updates throughout the afternoon. Dr. Gay let us know when the heart and lung machine was in place and the delicate operation had begun. The most important report came later, when the heart and lung machine was slowly removed, and Eric's heart miraculously began to beat again. The mood in the OR, SI and waiting room was one of cautious joy!

We'd been blessed throughout these last few months as people prayed for Eric and our family. Our church was one of the larger churches in Des Moines and our families lived close-by in smaller towns. Eric's name was known throughout the area, people were praying and there was evidence of answered prayer moment-by-moment. Even the local Christian radio station asked listeners to pray. They shared frequent updates during his surgery and recovery – people even called the station to ask about Eric!

Surgery is Over, Eric's Work Begins

Eric looked much better than after his previous surgery. I was familiar with the respirator and ready for it. Thankfully, he was dosed with pain meds, but slightly coherent and he knew we were there. I told him he had pink fingernails.

He tried to look, but his hands were restrained – a safety measure so IVs, drainage tubes, breathing tubes, etc. aren't pulled out. The evening was peaceful and the cardiologists and surgeons were thrilled with Eric's progress. His heart was strong, but he still needed the respirator.

I was grateful the staff kept a constant watch on Eric. This being the Surgical Intensive Care Unit, the operating rooms were close-by. The surgical team was in and out of Eric's room throughout the day. Even though I appreciated their constant observation, I was also a little amused and glad I wasn't the nurse taking the orders. The doctors gave various orders regarding Eric's care – by the hour - and each time it meant his nurse had to re-do this and un-do that or order a different medicine. At one point his nurse, in a professional tone and manner, read the list of doctors and orders to Dr. Gay with the question: "okay, so do you all agree?"

The Respirator

Eric spent more than a week in SI. Unlike the last surgery where he was extubated the next morning, this time, as a precaution, Dr. Gay kept him on the respirator. I absolutely trusted Dr. Gay's judgment and knew he was looking at bloodwork and Eric's EKG and listening to his heart and lungs. Watching my babe on a respirator was close to unbearable, however, he was still alive.

We had so many visitors and even though a bit exhausting to converse all day, they helped me maintain my faith and belief that Eric would make it. One evening I decided to sit in the OR waiting room and visit with a friend. Eric was content so I decided he'd be okay for a while. After maybe 15 minutes, his nurse found me and said that Eric was asking for something, but she couldn't understand him and he was getting frustrated. Eric was about five days post op so we were becoming familiar with life in the unit. When I got to him, he pointed to the breathing tube. I asked him a couple questions and he shook his head no. I was afraid to ask, but I was out of ideas... "Do you need the tube suctioned?" He shook his head "yes"!! Have you ever seen a breathing tube suctioned? The hose is detached from the respirator, saline solution is dribbled into the tube and a suction hose is threaded inside the tube to the trachea to draw secretions from the lungs. Eric gagged and thrashed in his bed whenever his breathing tube was suctioned, and yet, now he was asking to have it done. Until that moment I could hardly stand by as the breathing tube was cleaned. This five year old child had matured; he was willing to be "tortured" because obviously it made him more comfortable. After that, I settled with the respirator because Eric had.

We were now seven days post op and still on the respirator. This meant Eric wasn't strong enough to survive on his own. When I was asked for specific prayer requests, of course, I replied, "Please pray that Eric is weaned from the respirator!"

The primary heart surgeon and Dr. Gay hadn't completely agreed in regard to the respirator. The surgeon believed

Eric was ready to be extubated, but he respected Dr. Gay's caution (as did I), and therefore, Eric remained on the respirator.

It was late afternoon and most of the docs were gone for the day. Eric's nurse was arranging his bed and we rolled him onto his side for a change in positions. As we moved him, the breathing tube dislodged, and simultaneously, his heart surgeon walked into the room completely unaware of the sudden emergency! As soon as we alerted him, he removed the tube completely – and stayed awhile to monitor Eric's blood gases and watch how Eric tolerated it. Well, he not only tolerated it, he asked and I stress asked – out loud!! for ice chips!

A Visit from Lindsie!

One evening my grandparents brought Lindsie to the hospital. I had missed her so much, I was ecstatic to see her. All of my focus had understandably been on Eric, and Lindsie brought a welcome burst of energy and delight. I saw her from a distance and I hollered for her... when she saw me, she giggled and ran with out-stretched arms until she was three feet away... I was about to scoop her into my arms and she dodged to the right and ran to her uncle who was standing right behind me! What a little tease! I thought she was punishing me for being away. She'd spent so much time with my grandparents that eventually she didn't want to visit them at all because she was afraid I had to leave her again. Having to leave Lindsie to be at the hospital with Eric was heart breaking. It wasn't fair. I wanted to take care of both of my children, not leave one to care for the other. I consoled myself with knowing I had to be with the one who needed me most.

One Step Closer

Once Eric was off the respirator, his recovery picked up pace a bit and we soon returned to the peds floor.

A lot of patients have the misfortune of uncooperative veins when blood samples are drawn or IVs are started. In addition to this misfortune sometimes IVs infiltrate which is when a vein wears out and the IV solution begins seeping into surrounding tissue. That means another IV and another horrible session of finding a vein. This was always traumatic for Eric and for everyone within hearing distance, which was about 12 doors down the hall. As soon as staff came to the room, whether to start an IV or draw blood, Eric began to wail. The tech would give me a questioning look as to how many people we'd need to hold Eric down. My response was, "he makes a lot of noise, but he'll lay perfectly still." He did, every time and I was proud of him. I honestly felt that after all he'd been through, Eric earned the right to wail as loudly as he could!

The hospital had a way to help little patients, like Eric, who'd been on the receiving end of a lot of needles... a "therapy" doll the kids gave shots to using real needles and syringes. I can tell you that Eric really enjoyed giving the doll shots! Finally he was the shot-er rather than the shot-ee!

Sometimes Grammy and I took Eric for walks around the hospital in a wheelchair, with the IV pole closely in tow. Eric still had a urinary catheter collecting liquid gold - so the gold bag came along too! Eric took prednisone after all of his surgeries to treat the recurring Post Postpericardiotomy Syndrome. One of the side effects of prednisone was an increase in appetite – prednisone lived up to its reputation, Eric was ravenous. In addition to the meals served in his room, he was able to eat meals in the cafeteria and enjoyed the variety of food and getting out of his room. Many of those meals were a second lunch or a second supper; some days a second lunch and a second supper. I remember one of the trips to the cafeteria: just as we stepped out of the elevator, someone nearly walked between the wheelchair and the IV pole! He saw the IV line at the last split second and caught himself. Had he not, I think there'd have been a "code blue" call on me! It was one of those moments when you see it happening, you freeze, you hold your breath and you can't make a sound.

A med student made rounds one day with Dr. Gay. It was feeling like we might be going home soon. Nevertheless, of course, I was growing accustomed to the unexpected... Eric didn't need his pic line anymore and so the med student went to work removing it. Pic lines are stitched in place. Eric complained of it hurting enough that Dr. Gay took a closer look and suspected an infection around the site and inside the tubing. He began a ten-day IV antibiotic and had Eric's blood cultured. Thankfully, the infection wasn't staph. So here we were – another ten days in the hospital, but most importantly, the infection was caught early. The IV meds were given through a heparin lock catheter: the line was flushed with heparin and then plugged in to run the meds and unplugged the rest of the time. This meant Eric was not tethered to an IV pole. With our new freedom, we could easily leave the peds floor - the best part - minus an IV pole.

Hospital stays aren't all bad... Eric's sixth birthday was a couple weeks away so the hospital staff decided to have a birthday party for him. They spoiled us! Treats, balloon bouquets, stuffed animals. We were not only celebrating his birthday, but also the successful surgery! Again, we were blessed many times over by people who truly loved my son. He was familiar with nearly every department in the hospital from the lab to x-ray to physical therapy and the cafeteria! Even Dr. Gay's office staff came to Eric's party. Moments like this really do help to take some of the sting out of the rough times.

Grammy and Eric in Hospital

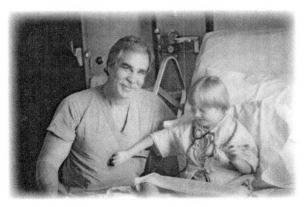

Eric Listening to Dr. Gay's Heart

Mommy and Eric at the Birthday Celebration

Living Life Again

We were finally released from the hospital. I was so
thankful that the April surgery was his last and now we
could actually live a normal life. It felt that an all-consuming

weight had finally been lifted, the black cloud hovering over us since Eric's birth, had blown away. God may not have healed him with a touch; He chose surgery. Either way Eric was a miracle.

Eric steadily gained strength and every step, though small, was encouraging. Eric's color had improved and the swelling was slightly better. However, the latest surgery caused fluid to collect in his abdomen, not just a little fluid, enough that he looked five to six months pregnant. Just like with pregnancy, sometimes that extra load was a challenge to carry, so Eric moved a bit slower. Because of the fluid buildup, Eric had to be placed on a fluid restriction. This was likely the most difficult, but necessary, piece to Eric's recovery. To add to it, Eric took meds that gave him a dry mouth. So the fluid restriction, coupled with the dry mouth, at times made my little boy extremely unhappy. One of the, somewhat cute, remedies Eric found: bath water. So Eric asked to take a lot of baths. Of course I knew he was drinking his bath water, but I didn't let him know that I knew! I didn't look the other way for long, just enough to give him a small break from the misery.

People innocently stared at Eric. His tummy was large and the rest of him frail. I never did, but always wanted to explain his appearance, but that would have hurt Eric. Another time wasn't so innocent... whenever I took my two kids to the mall, I carried Lindsie in a pouch and pushed Eric in the stroller. A very insensitive man looked at us, the older child riding and the younger in a pouch, and said "a little old for that isn't he?" I was appalled! And livid! I couldn't think quickly enough to say something in return. However, I've thought of plenty since and have concluded it was best that I was speechless at the time!

We had another celebration for Eric's sixth birthday, May 8. My grandma lived in an apartment building that had a nice community room we could use. Family and friends were invited to help celebrate his birthday. Eric was one month post op and seemed strong and ornery. As was his little sister – ornery that is.

It was a beautiful time of year! It was late spring, and after another Iowa winter, people were ready to enjoy the weather. In the winter, we wave at neighbors while hurrying to get in out of the cold. Springtime we get reacquainted. Everyone is happy! Eric played outside with all of his friends, our neighborhood was full of kids and they found plenty to do. One of our favorite family activities was bike riding with friends on trails around Saylorville Lake. Eric and Lindsie rode behind their dad in a "bugger" – so cute!

Summer started well for Eric even though the fluid retention in his face and abdomen persisted. In spite of it, Eric charged ahead. He enjoyed going to the pool and I decided it was time for swimming lessons. There was a day when he cried to get out of the water, that he was tired. I wanted him to learn to swim so I tried bribing him with a kid's meal from a fast food restaurant. He never turned down a kid's meal until that day. I didn't realize it then, but this was the beginning of a downhill slope.

The Tide Changed Again

A few days later Eric, Lindsie and I met friends at a local beach. My kids were raised at the beach year after year; they enjoyed it as much as I. Except for that day, Eric ran out of steam soon after we got there. I tried hard to talk myself out of what I saw hoping he was simply tired that day. I had asked Dr. Gay once how I'd know if Eric was in heart failure, he didn't list symptoms, he simply said, "you'll know."

It was July 4th and we went to watch our city's annual fireworks display. We sat with friends in the bed of a pickup in my grandparent's back yard. Eric lay with his head in my lap, he could barely lift it to watch the fireworks. That was not my Eric and it was time to face my denial and call the doctor. I was beginning to understand what Dr. Gay meant.

We met Dr. Gay's partner, Dr. Chandramouli, in the ER and Eric was admitted to the hospital. Dr. Chandra treated Eric with medications hoping a nonaggressive approach might get him back on track. Unfortunately, Eric didn't respond positively to the treatment, and again, it was becoming more apparent that heart failure was looming over us. The most difficult for me to watch was the nausea and vomiting, I felt so helpless. His arms and legs already bony, his body had nothing more to give.

Summer 1983

Dr. Gay had been out of town when Eric was admitted to the hospital. When he returned, Eric was scheduled for his sixth heart cath. I didn't realize how difficult the caths were on Eric until the night before when a nurse came to check on him and he awakened. He started crying, he thought it was time for the cath. We were sleeping together in a full size hide-a-bed and I held him close as I gently rubbed his back until he went back to sleep. If I could only take his place...

The heart cath revealed the need for another surgery, the third in 11 months. Eric's blood flow was hindered at the site of the previous operation and some minor reflux had developed as well. We stayed in the hospital until Eric's condition had stabilized enough that we could go home before the surgery.

We tried adapting our activities to accommodate Eric's limitations. We went for a bike ride; but the bugger was no longer fun. It broke my heart to ride behind him and see the look of misery on his face. He was nauseated and thirsty and the hot sun made it worse.

Movie theaters were better. We had a great time meeting some of the nurses from the peds floor and their kids to see Star Wars. We also went to ET with Grammy and Lindsie. The theater was sold out and we found seats in a back corner. Eric was completely engrossed in the movie; especially at the end when ET's heart stopped. The entire theater was silent when Eric let out a deafening cry that echoed from our back corner to the front far corner of the theater. I heard a lot of chuckling and when we left after the movie, a lady smiled and told her friend, "that's the little boy who cried."

Grandpa Al

There was a very special man who volunteered on the peds floor. We met him when Eric was in for his surgery in September 1982, Grandpa Al. Grandpa Al loved all of the kids and all of the kids loved him. He helped the staff whenever he could. He had a kindred spirit with the heart kids because he was a "heart kid" himself. Eric and Grandpa Al hit it off immediately and their friendship grew more each time Eric was back in the hospital. Not long before Eric's August 1983 surgery, Grandpa Al became very sick with cancer and underwent treatment at the hospital as well. When Grandpa Al heard that Eric was back for his third surgery in 11 months, he was very sad that he couldn't make it in to see Eric so he sent a friend in his place. He wanted Eric to know that he was praying for him and so sorry he couldn't be there himself. A few weeks later, Grandpa Al died of cancer. Grandpa Al was critically ill himself, but he worried more about Eric. Losing Grandpa Al left a void for everyone who knew him. I attended his funeral and was in awe to see the church overflowing with people whose lives Grandpa Al had touched. It was a fitting tribute to an amazing selfless man.

The Last Surgery

When we returned to the hospital, one of the nurses energetically asked, "What have you been doing all summer, Eric?" Eric's honest reply, "Vomiting." He told it like it was. Another time at the hospital someone asked him what kind of dog he had and he said "a mean one." It was fun to watch the reactions; usually the "asker" didn't know what to say!

Surgery the next morning got underway as usual. "As usual" shouldn't be a term associated with a six year old child especially when it comes to major surgeries. We should have been school shopping for his first day of kindergarten.

The same anesthesiologist from the April surgery attended this surgery, Eric was fading into a gentle, relaxed sleep as we parted. All of my beloved friends and family filled the waiting room like before. I was blessed.

The scar tissue wasn't as much of a hindrance as the April surgery so the day wasn't quite as long. We were able to see Eric midafternoon. This being Eric's third surgery in 11 months, the sight of him wasn't as devastating. While in his room in SI the doctors visited with us about his surgery. They discussed using a technique called circulatory arrest, something I'd never heard of, even though I'd signed a release the day before for circulatory arrest. Eric's head was packed in ice, his body temperature cooled and once all of his blood had collected in the heart and lung machine, the machine was turned off. Circulatory arrest enabled the surgeons to reach the area of Eric's heart that needed repair.

When I shared what the doctors told me about circulatory arrest I realized that, in a sense, Eric was clinically dead: no heartbeat, no oxygen. My dad thought out loud, "I wonder where his soul was?" Everyone agreed and sort of shrugged their shoulders and that was that. Until Eric told me a few weeks later...

Heaven

The Picture Eric Drew of Heaven's Gates

Eric and I were alone driving along Ashworth Road in West Des Moines; my grandma was going to keep Eric while I went to church, it was Sunday evening. I've never forgotten exactly when and where our first conversation took place. All of what's written here, Eric told me over the course of time. He truly spoke in a calm, what's-the-big-deal? sort of way.

"Mommy, where does Jesus live?" Eric asked.

"In our hearts and in Heaven." I answered.

"Well, where's Heaven?" he asked.

"I don't know, Eric." I replied.

"I do, I've been there." he said.

He said Jesus came to the operating room, took out his IV and respirator, they went out by the elevators and went up from there.

"We flew." he said.

"Did you fly in a space ship like Star Wars?" I challenged him.

"No like when Jesus died on the cross." he said emphatically.

I took that to mean they ascended. He told me about gates made of pearls.

"Were they pearls like Mommy's ring?" I asked.

"No, silver pearls." he said.

He offered to draw a picture: he drew arched open gates of pearls and he used a silver marker. I've always heard that the colors in Heaven are illuminated – pearls could have a silvery cast if they're illuminated. He also spoke of golden streets.

I asked his Sunday School teachers, Bible School teachers, all of his grandparents if they'd talked to Eric about Heaven and everyone gave the same answer, "No." Not only was I unable to find anyone who'd told Eric about Heaven, every detail of his story matched the Bible's account of Heaven. Nothing countered scripture; I couldn't shed doubt on anything he said.

What Eric told me next completely convinced me that what he was telling me was true. Remember, he was six years old. He had had four heart surgeries, his body was covered with scars from his neck to his ankles, I called them battle scars. He said he had a new body without scars. Eric had never ever mentioned the scars on his body and yet he noticed his new body in Heaven without scars. That convinced me.

> Another amazing thing he said, "I saw angels. They had wings that made noises."

I hadn't read the entire Bible at that time so I didn't know what he meant. However, I soon learned that he was referring to the four living creatures described in the first chapter of Ezekiel. Ezekiel said in verse one that the Heavens were opened and he saw visions of God. Later in verse 24, he spoke of the four living creatures that are in the Holy of Holies. Ezekiel goes on to say: and high above on the throne was a figure like that of a man.

Ezekiel. 1:24-28 (NIV)

"When the creatures moved, I heard the sound of their wings, like the roar of rushing waters, like the voice of the Almighty, like the tumult of an army.

Then there came a voice from above the vault over their heads as they stood with lowered wings. Above the vault over their heads was what looked like a throne of lapis lazuli (translucent blue), and high above on the throne was a figure like that of a man. I saw that from what appeared to be his waist up he looked like glowing metal, as if full of fire, and that from there down he looked like fire; and brilliant light surrounded him. Like the appearance of a rainbow in the clouds on a rainy day, so was the radiance around him.

This was the appearance of the likeness of the glory of the Lord. When I saw it, I fell facedown, and I heard the voice of one speaking."

I asked Eric if he had seen God. He said yes. In Exodus 33:20 The Bible says "for no one may see me and live." I thought, here's my chance...

"What does God look like?" I asked Eric.

"I can't tell you." he responded.

So being the authoritarian that I am I demanded, "Eric, I'm your mother, you tell me what God looks like."

He became equally stern with me and said, "I can't, you're not supposed to know."

He was obedient to God, not his mother. God knew in whom He could entrust His glory and holiness, who would honor Him and obey Him, even when his mommy prodded and pressured him!

I wrestled with what God said to Moses that no one could see Him and live, and as always, God responded so gently. He whispered the answer to my heart, "Lynn, Eric died." Not right then, but five months later.

Exodus 33:18-23 (NIV)

Then Moses said, "Now show me your glory."

And the Lord said, "I will cause all my goodness to pass in front of you, and I will proclaim my name, the Lord, in your presence. I will have mercy on whom I will have mercy, and I will have compassion on whom I will have compassion. But," he said, "you cannot see my face, for no one may see me and live."

Then the Lord said, "There is a place near me where you may stand on a rock. When my glory passes by, I will put you in a cleft in the rock and cover you with my hand until I have passed by. Then I will remove my hand and you will see my back; but my face must not be seen."

Paul also talked of being in the Holy of Holies. He said he heard things so astounding that he wasn't allowed to tell, that a man's mind can't comprehend. Eric did too. Paul also spoke of being caught up in the third Heaven. Whether in the body or out – he didn't know. Eric believed that Jesus came into the operating room and he physically got up from the table. I can't say if Eric's experience was a dream or a vision or if he was actually in Heaven – in spirit. Paul, in the following passage, also couldn't say if he was or wasn't physically in Heaven.

2 Corinthians 12:1-4 (NIV)

> *I (Paul) must go on boasting. Although there is nothing to be gained, I will go on to visions and revelations from the Lord. I know a man in Christ who fourteen years ago was caught up to the third heaven. Whether it was in the body or out of the body I do not know—God knows. And I know that this man—whether in the body or apart from the body I do not know, but God knows— was caught up to paradise and heard inexpressible things, things that no one is permitted to tell.*

In one of our conversations about Heaven, Eric said he saw a friend of mine, Ruth, who had died in a car accident about a year and a half earlier. Ruth was very beautiful not only outwardly, but inwardly. She lived every moment desiring more of God and less of herself. Whenever I was with Ruth, I was challenged to live life to a higher standard, a godly standard, the way she did. The last time I talked with her was to tell her about Eric's heart cath before the

September surgery. Ruth was killed on a Sunday morning on her way to church. Her car was filled with children, four of them her own and her twin brother, only Ruth died. The whole Christian community truly grieved for her. Many times throughout Eric's surgeries I thought of how I missed her.

When Eric saw Ruth in Heaven, he made special mention of the necklace she wore. Several months later, I met her mother, who was still grieving for her daughter. We sat at her kitchen table and I shared Eric's story and what he had told me about Ruth. When I spoke of the necklace, tears streamed down her face. The necklace had a special meaning and held a sentimental value between Ruth and her mom. I certainly can't explain the how and the why of the necklace. However, I do believe Eric was used to convey a sweet gift from God to Ruth's mom. It's always God's desire to comfort the brokenhearted.

Over the next several months whenever Eric talked of Heaven he was low key, he didn't consider it anything unusual. He showed more excitement over a pizza than a trip to Heaven. I have to admit that sometimes I got frustrated with him because I wanted to hear more and more about Heaven! I'd never known anyone who had gone to Heaven and come back to earth to tell about it! Also, I was a bit puzzled as to God's purpose in showing Eric all of Heaven when I was still clinging to the hope that Eric would recover, it was just a matter of time.

One evening as Eric and I watched Christian TV, a woman was being interviewed about her visit to Heaven. Like Eric, she was clinically dead, I can't recall if she was in an accident or was ill. While she was "dead" and before she was resuscitated, she went to Heaven. I could see Eric's face while she talked and he listened closely. After a few minutes he turned to me and asked, "Mommy, did I die?" Obviously he understood what happened to him and could relate to this woman's testimony, and again, he was six years old!

Eric was very different after his Heaven experience. He was peaceful and wise beyond his six years. Even when it came to the respirator, it was removed the morning after surgery. There was no excitement, one moment it was there and the next it was gone. Eric's food choices changed – seriously – he would choose a piece of fruit over a Snickers. I'd take the Snickers! One of his nurses in SI shook her head and said, "that's not a six year old in that bed."

Fall 1983

Dr. Gay prescribed medicine for Eric's nausea; he took it every morning before getting out of bed. When his stomach settled, he took the rest of his morning meds. Most of the time this helped get his day off to a good start.

Eric was well enough to attend school; after all, he was a kindergartner! We were blessed sending him to Des Moines Christian School; and doubly blessed because my parents helped with tuition. He missed the first few weeks of school, but most importantly, he made it! One day Eric told Grammy all about school and how much fun he had. He especially liked P.E. and described the different games. Knowing Eric couldn't participate, Grammy asked Eric what he did during class and he exclaimed, "I get to watch!"

1st Day of Kindergarten

I never heard Eric express self-pity at his circumstances and limitations. I think most children in their early years see themselves through an innocence that protects them from comparing themselves to their peers. The only time I'm aware that Eric compared himself to anyone was when he asked Grammy why Lindsie's heart wasn't like his. She gave him the most honest answer, she told him she didn't know. Another question Eric asked Grammy wasn't as difficult to answer, but sad all the same: he asked if Jesus could come into his heart... because his heart was sick? I have no doubt whatsoever, Jesus was already there.

Fluid Restriction and a Six Year Old

Eric was still on the fluid restriction. To add to that, he needed blood drawn once a week to monitor his electrolytes. Maintaining his electrolyte count was a battle between Lasix and his electrolytes, a catch-22:

Eric took the drug Lasix to help him lose the excess fluid
– when he'd lose the fluid
– his electrolytes became imbalanced
– when the electrolytes were imbalanced
– Lasix couldn't do its job
– So it was back to balancing the electrolytes.

Normally I took Eric to the hospital for the blood work before school, but one week I decided to wait until after school. Eric typically left school with a smile, but that day he walked out with a miserable look that usually meant he was nauseated. His teacher said that he'd felt sick all morning. Fear and anxiety had run away with him, he had worried all morning about the blood work planned for right after school. It broke my heart thinking about my sweet Eric worrying all morning and I was mad at myself for having such bad judgment. No matter how many IVs, shots, blood tests, he'd had he never took shots in stride. He was only six and needles hurt! I never delayed the blood test again.

I remember another rough day around that time when Eric had had enough of the fluid restriction. He was thirsty!! He wanted a drink!! Most of the time I tried to counsel Eric by explaining how certain things were beneficial and why he had to tough it out. That day I knelt down and was about to give another pep talk when I took a second and thought to myself, no, think of Eric's perspective, it had been a long and weary fight and he was tired. He began to cry and I took him into my arms and said, "Cry, Eric, cry. I don't blame you. Just cry." We stayed there a while, we were exhausted from the battle. As I write this I can still remember how he felt in my arms and how our hugs always seemed to make everything better.

And There were Good Days

Thankfully the bumpy days didn't completely rule. Eric was tough and he was determined to push aside the periodic hindrances so that he could do the things he enjoyed. Halloween, for one, was fun for Eric and Lindsie. Eric liked the Wizard of Oz and decided to dress-up as the wicked witch of the west, pointy hat and a long black robe. I couldn't talk him out of it. As a bonus, he did a great reenactment of melting into a heap on the floor. Lindsie was only two so I got to decide for her that she'd be a rock star! We hit several houses and had so much fun. Adel's beggar's night was the following night so we decided to go again. The second night didn't go so well for Lindsie though; she ate so much candy that she got sick!

Halloween: Witch & Rock Star

Eric's interests shifted to activities that were more sedentary. He decided he was a chef and created meals out of unusual ingredients: pickles, ketchup, potatoes. He was proud of his gourmet dishes and offered samples to everyone. He was most definitely on his way to cooking for a five star restaurant!

Heart Failure

One morning when I woke Eric for school, he didn't want to go. Even after taking his medicine, he still didn't want to go. With any other child you'd fear a flu bug or some other virus, but with Eric it couldn't be so easily dismissed. I kept him home, hoping maybe a day or two of rest and he'd get better.

Something new and peculiar was happening: one of Eric's arms swelled to nearly double its size. Once again, he had the doctors perplexed. They made some adjustments to meds and then came the distressing "wait and see" phase. But before that phase ended, we were back in the hospital. Eric was in heart failure again, or rather, still. It was never officially labeled as heart failure before then, but all the symptoms were there.

One symptom of heart failure is when fluid collects around the heart and lungs. This was obvious without a stethoscope or x-ray; Eric's labored and shallow breaths were enough evidence. One evening his breathing became critically labored, Dr. Chandra was on call and came to the hospital. Before he could get there, Eric's breathing worsened even more, so a doctor from the ER was called to the room. The ER doc monitored Eric's breathing and was able to wait for

Dr. Chandra. Once Dr. Chandra arrived, he quickly moved Eric to a treatment room. Dr. Chandra tapped Eric's lungs, which means he drew as much fluid out of the pleural sac as possible with a large syringe inserted between Eric's ribs and into the pleural sac; finally Eric's breathing significantly improved and he rested more comfortably. He was given electrolytes through an IV and now the Lasix would be able to keep the fluids at a manageable level.

This hospital stay lasted a couple weeks, longer than I expected because Eric didn't have surgery. It had gotten to the place that if friends couldn't reach me at home, they called my second home, the hospital. We were kept awhile so the docs could regulate meds and keep electrolytes balanced. Eventually we got to the place when Dr. Gay said "we're not doing anything for him here that you can't do at home."

I wasn't ready to accept that my son may die. God had brought us through so much and had answered prayers from an army of prayer warriors. I clung to my faith that Eric would be whole, whether immediately or gradually I didn't know, but he was going to live a strong and healthy life… after we got through all of this.

A Brief Respite

After the fluid had been drained from around his lungs and his electrolytes stabilized, Eric felt a little stronger. The nausea medication also helped. It appeared we might finally be headed down the right path, but we had learned to tread cautiously.

The Kingdom Heirs had a Christmas concert at the Methodist Church in Adel. I shared Eric's story with the congregation and Eric got to sing the song "Come on Ring Those Bells" with the Kingdom Heirs. This had been his dream and all those imaginary concerts of singing into pretend microphones came to fruition that morning! Grammy bought him a gray sweater vest, shirt and pants, a red bow tie, and his favorite - burgundy cowboy boots. Eric beamed as he sang his song and he looked so healthy, the fluid in his face and abdomen still held at bay with the help of meds. Eric's health since July 4th had seemed to be on a roller coaster, an exhausting roller coaster, but maybe – just maybe, we'd turned a corner.

The Sunday Eric Sang with the Kingdom Heirs

Eric and Lindsie

One Last Option...

Eric's respite was brief. The fluid crept back and we found ourselves on a downhill plunge. Eric's seventh heart cath was scheduled for Monday, December 11, it was also my mom's birthday. Dr. Gay called on Saturday morning before the cath to tell us that there had been a discussion about one last option for Eric. Rather than discuss it over the phone, he invited us to his home that afternoon. From the way Dr. Gay sounded and that he wanted us to go to his house, it must be something drastic.

The heart team had contacted an associate of Dr. Christiaan Barnard, the South African heart surgeon who was the first surgeon to successfully perform an adult human heart transplant and piggyback heart transplant. This was before children had undergone heart transplants. However, a complete heart transplant wasn't being discussed, but rather, a piggyback heart transplant. As I suspected, this was radical. I couldn't read Dr. Gay, was he recommending it or was he simply fulfilling his professional obligation to communicate all possible options for Eric?

The piggyback transplant would mean adding a second heart to support Eric's diseased heart. His body would have two hearts working together: the new heart picking up the slack for his own heart. The operation would likely draw national media attention, if not international media attention and much of it unfavorable. If we chose to go forward with it, we'd have to be steadfast in our decision and able to withstand criticism. I asked if there were other child piggyback heart transplant recipients that I could talk with; to ask if they'd recommend having the transplant and what their experiences had been. There were none, Eric would be the first. After a lengthy and thorough discussion, Dr. Gay told me to discuss it with our families and we'd talk again on Monday.

No one in either family, mine or my in-laws, was receptive to the idea of a piggyback heart transplant. I have to say that I wasn't as set against it as everyone else, but I would abide by their decision. On the other hand, the thought of putting Eric through such a drastic procedure, I knew was selfish; I was groping at anything to keep my son alive. I tried to sense what Eric would choose if he were older and could make the decision himself. Saying no to the transplant meant we were choosing death unless God intervened. Dr. Gay's words were again appropriate... "I don't want to be pessimistic, but I have to be realistic."

The heart cath revealed that Eric's heart was in an acute stage of heart failure. The heart team had depleted every possible option and we were told that in a matter of time, Eric would die. The black cloud that had blown away eight months earlier was back. This time it wasn't hovering, it consumed me.

We told Dr. Gay that we had decided against the piggyback heart transplant. Eric had already been through so much and, though it was extremely difficult, it was time to say "enough." I sensed that Dr. Gay agreed with our decision. Choosing death for my six year old son will always be my life's lowest low and darkest moment.

Eric and Dr. Gay

We stayed in the hospital a few more days to get Eric's electrolytes balanced and to have the fluid drained from around his lungs. I remember a sweet moment between Eric and Dr. Gay: Eric asked him to remove the fluid restriction. Dr. Gay's initial response was no, but it was how he said it... "Eric, I'm talking to you like you were my own." I think Eric understood because the next thing he asked Dr. Gay was for money to go to the gift shop!

Laura Lynn Sargent

Dr. Gay had been Eric's doctor from the time Eric was a day old. He had just moved to Des Moines to start his pediatric cardiology medical practice and Eric was one of his first patients. Over the past year, we'd been in contact almost daily and the relationship had evolved into a friendship as well as doctor/patient. I was always thankful for Dr. Gay, and without a doubt, his concern for Eric was genuine.

Soon after the conversation about the fluid restriction, Dr. Gay decided it was time for Eric to get his wish and he removed the fluid restriction. Sadly, the reason wasn't because Eric was well enough, but rather, to give him some pleasure in his last days. A few weeks earlier Eric had told his grammy that he "just knew" he'd be off the fluid restriction by Christmas. When he saw her later that morning he exclaimed with delight, "See, I told you I'd be off the fluid restriction by Christmas!" Bittersweet.

Coping with Reality

Nightmares are vivid and waking up from a nightmare you immediately assure yourself it was just a dream; it wasn't real; you shake it off and go back to sleep. The night following Eric's heart cath, I had a dream that he had died. In my dream, an unbearable all-consuming sense of mourning bore down on me; I wanted so badly to break free, but it had me trapped. This is the worst nightmare a mother can have. I couldn't dismiss it because I knew it was a glimpse of what lay ahead. The nightmare stayed with me and no matter how much I tried, I couldn't forget it.

One of my pastors stopped by the hospital as he did quite often; we'd become close over the previous year and a half. He had a tender soothing way about him and I'd grown to love him like a dad. We talked about coping with broken hearts like mine and he went on to say that many people in my place become angry at God. What he didn't know was that I was one of those people. I was angry at God, but I didn't tell Pastor Don. He said it is a choice and we can choose to be angry or we can choose a soft heart so that God can comfort us. I wasn't ready for that, my Bible was collecting dust, I was mad at God and preferred to ignore Him.

The next day, for some reason, I made a quick trip home from the hospital. I didn't go home often. When Eric was in the hospital, I was in the hospital. This afternoon I was home alone. I sat on my couch and talked to God. Actually, I didn't talk to Him, I was furious with Him. I felt He had been cruel in allowing Eric to go through all of the surgeries and heart caths, all of the painful procedures, all of the emotional highs and lows. He let Eric defy death so many times and we found encouragement believing God was answering all of our prayers, but now He was letting Eric die! I yelled as loudly as I could; "What good are You? Eric went through all of this and now You are going to let him die? In the future, if I need something, I'll ask You for the opposite because that's what You've given me." God let me unleash my wrath, He's got strong shoulders, He held me close and listened and waited patiently for me to exhaust my rage. Then in His tender way, He simply loved me back. I had never before experienced God's love like I did that afternoon. It was a new facet of His character to me and it made me love Him more. It didn't matter how angry I was or how disrespectful I was; God returned my fury with His unconditional love. I didn't deserve His compassion and grace, but God never gives us what we deserve. His love isn't in response to anything we do, His love is who He is all the time. That afternoon I chose to soften my heart and let God comfort me and wipe away my tears. Even though I didn't understand why God was letting Eric die, I trusted Him because He is sovereign and He knows the end from the beginning. *2 Corinthians 1:3&4 ... Blessed be the God and Father of our Lord Jesus Christ, the Father of mercies and God of all comfort.*

Mended Hearts Christmas

Mended Hearts is a support group for anyone who's had heart surgery. Every year they have their Christmas party at the hospital and invite children who've had heart surgery. We'd gone to the party since Eric was a baby. One year a reporter and photographer from a local TV station came to the Christmas party to do a story for that evening's news. Of course, Eric wanted to be on TV; he tagged along behind the crew until the reporter finally gave in and interviewed him!

Dr. Gay played Santa every year at the Mended Hearts Christmas party. One year Eric became suspicious that Santa was really Dr. Gay. "He has Dr. Gay's eyes." Eric confronted him at our next office visit, and after giving it some thought, Dr. Gay told Eric the truth that, yes, he was Santa and that it was "their secret." The Christmas party was only a week or two away and Eric grinned all through the party because he and Santa had a secret!

We were still in the hospital when the annual Mended Hearts Christmas party rolled around. This Mended Hearts party was a difficult one. Eric went to the party in a wheelchair and wearing his robe and hospital pajamas, far from the Eric who pestered the news team to be on TV. I watched him sit on Santa's lap for the last time. As I watched, the reality of what would soon happen filled my mind, I wasn't sure how I would go on without my Eric babe.

Santa and Eric

Eric's Last Mended Hearts Christmas Party

Earlier that evening, Eric asked Grammy if they could go to the gift shop. All he wanted was to buy a Christmas card for Lindsie – his "sistie." He wrote a note to Lindsie in the card and sealed the envelope. Grammy decided to keep it until Lindsie was old enough for it to mean something to her. Grammy gave it to Lindsie when she turned 13, the card said simply "Love, Eric."

Christmas

For the next month our focus was on keeping Eric comfortable; the fluid retention and nausea were nearly impossible to conquer. Almost weekly, the oral medications became ineffective, therefore, it was back to the hospital to have Eric's lungs tapped followed by an overnight stay for electrolytes intravenously. Eric was sedated when his lungs were tapped, and thankfully, he never complained that it hurt.

A cute memory I have from one of those short visits was the night I watched my weekly episode of "Knots Landing" at the hospital. Eric thought the name of the show was "Slops Landing." I decided that maybe he had better judgment than I!

Christmas season was bittersweet; that word again. Eric had his ups and downs. One evening he was strong enough to help make Christmas goodies. He was still a practicing chef, you know. He was able to be with me in the kitchen all evening; it went without saying, we cherished our time together. I wanted so much for that night to be a turning point that Eric was on his way back. I always looked for a ray of hope, but it never came.

I don't remember many details about Christmas 1983 other than Eric was very sick. There must have been a blizzard because my brother, Lee, had trouble getting home. I don't remember the blizzard, but I remember my brother becoming stranded. At that time of his life, he was a DJ on a radio station in north central Iowa. We all knew we were likely facing Eric's last Christmas, and so Lee, determined to be with his nephew, set out on snowy roads. He didn't even make it halfway. He spent Christmas Eve at a farmhouse with a typical Iowa farm family who opened their home to Lee and other stranded Christmas travelers. By Christmas Day the roads had improved enough that Lee made it safely home.

Eric had a half-sister who lives in North Carolina; she moved there when she was in elementary school. Her name is Donna Lea. She was seven years older than Eric. They didn't get to see each other as often as we'd have liked, but they were bonded together all the same. Their love and loyalty was unbreakable. Whenever Eric was asked how many siblings he had, Donna was never passed over. Thankfully, Donna Lea was in town for a short visit at Christmas; it was the last time she saw her brother. She put a spark in Eric that I hadn't seen for weeks.

As I mentioned earlier, we were in continual communication with Dr. Gay. He told us to call him anytime throughout the Holidays if Eric needed him. In the middle of it all, Dr. Gay broke his leg - a serious spiral break! He was ice skating with his children, I think he should have been inside fixing cocoa. When we found out about the accident, Eric and I decided it would be appropriate to take Millie's tenderloins to the Gays. We also thought it appropriate to stay and eat a tenderloin with them!

Dr. Gay didn't follow doctor's orders... he continued to manage Eric's care. He could have given orders over the phone, but he came to the hospital to care for Eric. He leaned on his crutches as he drained the fluid from around Eric's lungs. The look on his face was of intense pain, but no one could have stopped him when it came to Eric. Eric signed Dr. Gay's cast and I was told that later, when his cast was removed, he kept the portion with Eric's signature.

Going home...

Eric showed no signs of improvement, undeniably he was slipping away. People who came to visit could see drastic changes in him. It wasn't as noticeable to me because I was with him day after day. He began spending all of his time in bed or lying on the couch. He was weak; his voice was barely audible. Nausea continued to leave Eric with no pleasures in this life. His breathing became more labored, especially at night. I asked him to pray with me for healing, but he wouldn't. His refusal made me wonder if he already knew that God would soon call him home, that possibly he was told on that August day when he went to Heaven? I didn't ask him because I was afraid he might say "yes."

Shortly after Christmas, Eric's dad and I prayed together asking God to either heal Eric or call him home. Most of all, we prayed that God wouldn't leave Eric like he was. Not long after our prayer Eric's kidneys began to shut down.

I can only speak for myself, but I've seen situations where God allows time for us to selflessly let go of our loved one before death. Eric's dad and I let go when we prayed together. We put Eric in God's hands, asking for healing, but willing to lose him rather than watch him suffer.

We went into the hospital on a Monday for what we thought was another stay to tap Eric's lungs and replenish his electrolytes. This time he didn't respond like he had in the past. A drainage tube was left in place, but his lungs filled faster than they drained.

As word spread that we were losing Eric, our Christian friends came to the hospital. Some prayed with us, some came just to offer love and we were thankful for everyone who reached out to us. Thursday, the day before Eric died, we had a steady line of visitors from 7:30 in the morning until 9:00 that evening. My mom and his Grandma Ruth stayed with Eric while his dad and I met visitors.

Thursday night, my mom and I both stayed with Eric. He still had an IV and was able to get out of bed to use the bathroom, but he needed help. Toward morning, Eric asked for a pain pill. When his nurse brought the pill, he reached for it, but had trouble finding the pill in the nurse's hand. That was the moment my mom realized that when God told her Eric would go home on Friday, He meant Heaven. She was the last one to let go. God had been so very patient with her.

Early Friday morning we moved to a larger hospital room. I decided that I wouldn't leave Eric, that I'd be by his side all day. It was the right decision because visitors came about ten minutes before his death; if I'd left the room to visit with them, I might not have been there when he died.

Eric's kidneys had completely shut down and the swelling in his body grew worse. Breathing became more difficult so he was given medication to ease his discomfort. I knew the end was close. Eric had a favorite Maranatha Praise song. Whenever he heard the song on the radio, he'd close his eyes, raise his hands and worship and he always tilted his face and looked toward Heaven with the sweetest expression on his face. I had the song on tape and set it to repeat. As Eric grew weaker, his song continued to play. The very last thing I said to Eric was "I love you." He whispered back his last words, "I love you, too." The song played and I know Eric worshipped and as he did, he grew closer and closer to God. When his spirit actually left his body, I don't think he even knew – he entered Heaven singing "Let's forget about ourselves and magnify the Lord and worship Him."

I know without a doubt that Eric's last breath on earth was not his last breath. God, in His infinite wisdom, called Eric home. I know that God sees death from both sides; we only see death from this side of Heaven. What more could God have done for me than to take Eric to Heaven, and then bring Eric back to tell me about Heaven, before He called him home? I believe that Eric's experience in Heaven wasn't as much for him as it was for me and all of us. God wants us to know where Eric is, and in knowing, we will find comfort for every moment of every day and night until God calls us home, too.

Home from the Hospital

When I returned home, after Eric's death, two of my mom's closest friends were waiting, Jayne and Betty. I walked through my front door and into their arms; I was so thankful that they were there. Betty had lost her oldest daughter to cancer and she was close to Eric's age when she died. Betty said that she believed God had blessed them in special ways since their daughter's death. Her tone was so tender and comforting. She also talked of how, over the years, her grief healed and eventually her little girl had become a sweet memory. I couldn't imagine Eric becoming a sweet memory because at that moment it hurt too much.

I listened to a Dallas Holmes song, "I Saw the Lord." The song is about Heaven and seeing the Lord in Heaven and just the awe of it. I thought about Eric in Heaven only a few hours and that I wouldn't ask him to leave Heaven to come back. He was safe where there is no pain and he had a new body "without scars."

The house began to get busy. I was thankful because I wasn't ready to face the quiet. My grandparents brought Lindsie home. She was aware that something had happened to Eric, but too little to understand. As soon as she stepped inside the door, she demanded to see Eric. She didn't see him downstairs so she charged over to the stairs thinking he must be upstairs. She wouldn't accept answers from anyone, she was determined to find Eric. I tried to hold her and console her, but it was useless. Eventually she was distracted by all the activity and quieted down, but that wasn't the last of it.

The conversations were a brief distraction, somewhat helpful, in keeping my mind on something other than my broken heart. I caught myself laughing a few times until I remembered I had just lost Eric. I thought, "How could I laugh right now?" and then became irritated with myself. I rarely displayed emotion around people; I could always sense when I was about to break down so I'd find a private place to be alone and cry.

"Business" of the Funeral

The next morning, we went to the funeral home to plan services. The most difficult part was picking out a casket. I sat in the funeral home office and looked around wondering, "how did I get here? ...this can't be real." I had trouble grasping the reality that I was choosing a casket for my son, my son, who was just with me yesterday, and today he's gone. Had it not been for God's closeness, I couldn't have completed the "business" of my son's funeral. The fog around me lifted enough to choose a little white casket. Eric would wear his new red bowtie, gray sweater vest, shirt and pants and his new cowboy boots. The clothes he wore a month earlier to sing with the Kingdom Heirs.

Visitation

Sunday was Eric's visitation. The family met an hour before it began so that we could view Eric's body in the casket, privately. I was thankful for the time to get over the initial shock, a mother should never have to stand next to her child's casket, ever. Most of it, honestly, was surreal. I found myself touching, caressing, and kissing Eric's face; something I'd never done to a body nor have I done since. He was my son and it came naturally. Throughout the afternoon, I returned to the little white casket again and again. Before the casket was shut for the last time, the funeral home staff snipped a lock of Eric's hair for me. Our hair color was uncommon and a perfect match. I have always regretted that I didn't keep the little burgundy cowboy boots; so many things you don't think through, especially at such a time as that.

The rest of the day was full of blessings and tears. So many people came. One girlfriend I hadn't seen in years cried as she attempted to comfort me. She was upset with herself, saying she wanted to be strong for me. I told her, and I meant it, her tears touched me more than anything she could have said.

People don't always attend funerals or visitations because they don't know what to say and they're afraid of saying the wrong thing. Being there meant more to me than words. I still recall many who came to Eric's visitation, but what they said has long been forgotten.

Most of the afternoon my grandma sat alone in a chair close to Eric's casket and shook her head; like the rest of us, it was too much for her to grasp. Eric was the first death in our family and that included my brother, grandparents, aunts and uncles and all of my cousins on both sides. No one was even sick. So to say that this shook our family, is an understatement, there had never been anything more heartbreaking.

Those who Came to the Funeral of a Child

Eric's funeral was Monday morning. I will never forget the little white casket that sat at the front of the church. The service was powerful and the solo "We Shall Behold Him" perfectly fit the message preached about a little boy who at that very moment was again "beholding" his God face-to-face.

The church sanctuary was filled with people; some I didn't even know. People who had prayed for Eric; and loved the little boy with strawberry blonde hair and freckles. This was the only church he'd ever attended: Sunday School, Bible School, Pre-School and pretty much any other time the doors were open. I thought back to the Sunday he'd been baptized; when he climbed into the water, he completely disappeared from the congregation's sight. I'll never forget how he came out of the water smiling that contagious smile of his, and this time, the joy went clear to his toes!

Eric died on Friday afternoon, and with the funeral being Monday, there wasn't enough time for Des Moines Christian School to cancel classes. That had been their intent, and just knowing it, was huge to me. Earlier in the fall, the teachers and students had set aside a day to fast and pray for Eric. It wasn't mandatory, of course, but optional. Eric had only attended school for a short time, so their selfless gesture meant even more.

Dr. Gay and Dr. Chandra closed their office so their staff could attend Eric's funeral. Also, nearly every department throughout Mercy Hospital was represented. I think Eric won the hearts of so many because of the longevity of his hospital stays and he defied death over and over again. Each time he'd turn the corner, the staff let themselves become more vulnerable to love Eric.

Then, there was Missy. Missy lived across the street from us; and she loved Eric and he loved Missy. Missy was going to marry Eric and she meant it. They went to church together; pre-school together and Bible school together. They rode on the church van to Bible school. Evidently, the van went to two small towns close-by: Norwalk and Waukee. Eric said they went to Norwaukee. As Eric became too weak to play, Missy would ask her mom if she could still come over to our house. Her mom would press her a little knowing Eric couldn't play anymore and Missy said, "But I can still be with him." And she did. At Eric's funeral, Missy couldn't be consoled, but how could she? They were best friends. In the years that followed, whenever she had a writing assignment in school, Missy wrote about Eric. She still remembers his birthday and she still remembers January 13. She now has three kids of her own and her youngest son's middle name is Eric. I will always love Missy.

Scott

A little boy named Scott also came to Eric's funeral. Scott knew Eric from Sunday School and Des Moines Christian School. Our families had only recently met at church through the boys. It was especially important to Scott and his family to attend Eric's funeral. Six months later, Scott was diagnosed with an adrenal carcinoma tumor, a very rare and aggressive cancer. He had immediate surgery and a tumor the size of a football was removed. He underwent aggressive treatment to no avail. Scott died a few weeks later; those few weeks were way too short.

Before Scott passed, his parents took him home where he was more comfortable. I didn't know if I should visit because my son had died and Scott's family was still clinging to the hope that God would heal their precious son. However, my pastor encouraged me to go. Scott's mom, Cheryl, and I became dear friends through it all.

Just hours prior to Scott's death, he told his mom about seeing beautiful flowers. He said, "The flowers are so much prettier and brighter than anything we have here and the streets are really bright gold." In their conversation, his mom mentioned Eric, and Scott's reply was, "He's here." After looking up at his parents and telling them he loved them, Scott's last words were, "I've got to go now." Heaven was so close and real.

God reached out again to me, and now Cheryl, through our sons. He wants us to know without a doubt that our sons are in Heaven. This big God who's got a whole universe to care for, took time for Scott, Eric, and their moms and He's got time for us all. He wants to be known by us; He pursues us through His grace and mercy.

Grief

How does a mother go on after her child dies? Everything hurts – everything. There are no words to truly describe how it feels to lose a child; people asked me and my reply, "For a moment a mother can imagine her child's death. I did. Only for a moment, because even that moment is more than we can take in and we quickly, understandably push it away. When your child dies, there's no pushing it away; sorrow and mourning have a paralyzing grip on you that makes each moment of your life a burden, a burden too much to bear."

For a long time, my mind relived the last week of Eric's life: every Monday I relived his last Monday, every Tuesday I relived his last Tuesday and on, every detail. On Fridays I relived the day Eric died, hour-by-hour and down to moment-by-moment. How could he have just been here and now he was gone? Gone. I wanted to go back and hold him, talk to him, hear his voice, his last whisper, "I love you, too."

Many times I tried to figure out how the world could keep going as if nothing had happened. I mean, didn't they know that my son died? I wanted to scream "stop! it hurts!" But the world didn't stop and wouldn't stop and even if it had, that wouldn't have brought Eric back.

Living day-to-day in itself became an effort because Eric and Lindsie were my day-to-day, my all. I had dreamed of them for years, even before they were born. I wanted both of my children. They each have their own place in my heart and now my heart hurt with an ache that I was sure would never end. How could it? If I ever got to that place, would I forget Eric? Would he become a passing thought? Never, he was every thought, every breath, but he wasn't here anymore.

Nighttime was the worst. I had been prescribed sleeping pills, but I tried to keep from taking them every night. I stayed up and watched late night TV hoping that I'd get tired enough to go right to sleep once I went to bed. That only happened when I took the pills. Somehow, darkness seemed to magnify everything that hurt. The thought I couldn't turn off most was Eric's death, as peaceful as it was, but the night did its best to force me to relive his death night after night after night.

Darkness also brought on other disturbing thoughts... when I heard the ice cold January wind outside my window I worried about Eric in the grave, that he'd get cold. I never let my kids get cold: they had down filled coats for outdoors and they slept in two sleepers on cold nights (a light weight sleeper under a blanket sleeper). I knew Eric wasn't in the grave, but with the black night and fierce wind haunting thoughts overcame me. I wasn't detaching Eric's spirit from his body. As God is always faithful, I found strength in *2 Corinthians 5:1 "For we know that if the earthly tent we live in is destroyed, we have a building from God, an eternal house in heaven, not built by human hands."* Many times it took effort on my part to let scripture, the Sword of the Spirit, go to battle for me, when I persevered, God's peace and strength carried me again.

My first waking thought every morning was, "it really happened, he died." As I think about it, Eric had been my first thought every morning since he was conceived. I had to pry myself out of bed, and had it not been for Lindsie, I probably wouldn't have. Things I routinely did, I had to consciously make myself do: such as brushing my teeth, getting dressed, getting Lindsie dressed. Life's everyday details took more effort than I had.

Girlfriends kept me busy, and for a couple hours, it seemed to help mask my yearning for Eric. They invited me to lunch, and if it wasn't that, I kept busy in other ways. Maybe if I went hard enough I could outrun my inconsolable heart, and therefore, have less idle time to feel. It didn't work. Every waking moment was drenched with an overwhelming sorrow.

This went on for several weeks until I caught the flu. I had no choice, I was on my back for three days. It wasn't the flu that produced the most misery, it was the stopping, and stopping meant I had to face my shattered existence. In the quiet, it didn't take long to realize I wasn't alone. God had been waiting for me to slow down and let Him walk me through my grief – little by little – He knew exactly what

I was ready to confront and that's what we did. And while we did, God comforted me like only He can.

I realized that my healing needed to go slowly because the depth of my pain was vast. I didn't want to let any memory, any hurt slip through God's fingers as He gently gathered the tiny slivers of my life. Eric was worthy of every tear, every ounce of sorrow I experienced; I would let go gradually and in God's time. I prayed out of desperation that God would hold me in one arm and Eric in His other arm, I don't know how, but I know He did.

One Sunday during an evening church service, I had an especially intimate experience with God. As we sang the Maranatha praise song "I Love You, Lord" I sensed a beautiful closeness to God, and as I did, I thought of Eric also worshipping this very same Father God at this very same moment. I couldn't see Eric in Heaven and he couldn't see me on earth, but God saw us both, and in a sense, that's where we met with God in the middle. My heart still sings, "I Love You, Lord!"

Little Sister

While I was consumed in my own sorrow, I nearly missed Lindsie's. Being 2 ½, Lindsie was old enough to know something had happened to Eric, but too little to understand death. Whenever we drove past a building that slightly resembled the hospital, she asked if we were getting Eric. Once my mom was sick and Lindsie feared Grammy was dying. This went on for a while and I did my best to explain Eric's death to her and that he was in Heaven, but it never satisfied her. She became more frustrated each time.

One evening Lindsie and I watched a movie on television called "Six Weeks." It is about a young girl dying of leukemia. Lindsie picked up immediately that the girl was dying and asked why. I did my best to explain leukemia to her, but she kept asking why. The more she asked the more upset she got. I turned the channel, but that upset her even more and she started crying! So I turned back to the movie. The why's and tears kept up until I quit trying to explain leukemia and said, "I don't know why, Lindsie, I don't know why she's dying." And it was the truth. With that, Lindsie stopped asking. She continued to cry; I held her and rocked her until she cried herself to sleep. After that night, she seemed better, less angry; I felt she was beginning to heal.

Memories at Home

Not long after Eric died, I went through his bedroom. It was painful to look at his toys and clothes and his empty bed. I gathered his clothes into my arms trying to breathe in the scent of him. There was play dough in the carpet. When it happened, I tried every cleaning remedy I could find to remove it with no success, but after Eric died, it gave me a bittersweet sense of comfort and I was thankful the play dough was still there. There were a lot of notebooks with pages of pictures he'd drawn and notes he'd written and signed. Then I found his tape recorder and several cassette tapes. I listened to each one and the last one I found was the most amazing gift, a hidden treasure. Eric had recorded a love letter to his family. He listed his family members, embellishing a bit on each one. I was amazed that he'd accomplished this without me hearing him, I had no idea the tape existed until that day after his death. I prayed a prayer to praise God, I knew something this beloved could only have been arranged by Him.

Thankfully, Lindsie wore a lot of Eric's clothes and played with the same toys. I didn't have to make a decision as to what to do with his things. Strangely, I found that comforting. By the time Lindsie had outgrown the toys and clothing, they were no longer Eric's, they were hers. I am thankful I didn't give away any of Eric's belongings because if I'd done it too soon, in my emotional state, I might have given away something I cherish now.

So many things I didn't anticipate... Eric's empty chair at the dinner table. The weekly laundry; I missed his clothes. I found a used tissue in the pocket of his winter coat; I left it because he'd touched it last... Maybe if I closed my eyes and thought long and hard enough I could go back to the day he put it there and change everything. Crazy, I know, death does that.

Grief is Lonely

I found losing Eric to be lonely, and of course, it should have been; I don't want anyone to experience the loss of a child. I tried not to be, but I was envious of my friends who had all of their children and my son had died. This is hard for me to admit, because these feelings were solely mine. None of my friends excluded me. In fact, my girlfriends were a tremendous support in that they were always ready to listen when I needed to talk. However, they truly didn't know exactly what I was experiencing: the little things and the all-consuming giants and the gaping hole that used to be my heart. They didn't understand that grief was woven into every fiber of my being; they weren't intimate with death like I was forced to be. I didn't want to burden my friends with the moment by moment sorrow that had overtaken me so I kept so many thoughts quiet and continued to feel alienated.

The one person I could talk to any time of the day or night was my mom. We've always been close and Eric brought us even closer. Mom carried this grief with her as deeply as I did. She was the one who spent day after day and hour after hour at the hospital with me and for me so I could rest. As I've already said, her sadness was twofold: she grieved for the Eric she loved and she hurt for me. This time there wasn't a simple mom fix like putting a band aide on my skinned knee or standing over me wiping my forehead with a cool rag when I was sick. This was getting down in the trenches. We both learned how being a mom is the greatest joy in life until it became the greatest sorrow. My mom was my example of a godly woman; she lives her faith every day without faltering. She and I together remembered the holidays and the other dates on the calendar that were significant to only Eric, and together, gradually we healed.

Remember my friend, Bambi, who'd shared the scripture from Psalms before Eric's surgery? Mom, Lindsie and I were at her house for lunch shortly after Eric died, her three kids and Lindsie played close-by. As we visited, out of the corner of my eye, like always, Eric was in the pack, I thought... until I remembered he wasn't. I didn't have two kids anymore. Lapses like this didn't happen often, but when they did, snapping back to reality was a hard blow.

Things Unexpected

I knew that stopping in Eric's classroom at the Christian School would be difficult, but it turned out to be even more so than I expected. Des Moines Christian had a waiting list and a new student had taken Eric's place. It was apparent that life on earth had moved on, but I hadn't. I forced a smile while my insides turned to shreds.

I didn't expect the annual excitement of the last day of school to have an impact on me, it did. I thought about Eric's kindergarten class and how he should be there, too, but healthy and full of life. Nor did I think about Memorial Day; it had always been a happy day to barbeque and celebrate the start of summer; now I went to the cemetery to decorate Eric's grave, what a contrast.

Facing all of the firsts was unbearable: especially Christmas; there was no escaping Christmas, it was everywhere. Before Eric died, I enjoyed everything about Christmas; especially sharing it with my kids. After he died, I wanted to take a sleeping potion and awaken after the New Year. Christmas was distressing enough on its own, and with the memories of Eric's last Christmas, it was insurmountable. Sadly, it took several years to enjoy Christmas again.

My mind never gave me a break from relentlessly searching back through every holiday, birthday and season to find memories of Eric. But yet, I wanted to, I needed to draw those memories to the surface and hold them in my heart again, while cherishing each detail. It wasn't just the dates on the calendar, I also found that every restaurant, store, park, and everywhere else I went, I thought back to a time when Eric was there with me. Even the anniversary of his surgeries; I looked back in awe of Eric's bravery, but also his struggles and the pleading in his eyes for me to help when I couldn't do anything at all. These days were bittersweet to relive; there was no avoiding them because my mind was compelled, determined, to take me there.

Sacrifices

Even though I was with Lindsie, I wasn't with Lindsie. She was robbed of her mother's attention. I surely didn't want to drift away, but I was away. Lindsie was 13 months old when Eric had the heart cath in August of 1982. I was still nursing her and didn't want to stop, but when we came home after the hospital stay, she wouldn't nurse. I enjoyed nursing her; it was priceless time that belonged to only Lindsie and me. With hospital stays from August 1982 through January 1984 – we were in the hospital as much as we were home. Again, Lindsie was "pushed" aside. To be with one child, I had to be away from the other. Everyone sacrificed something. Sadly, once I could be with Lindsie, Eric was gone.

I hurt for Lindsie because she no longer had Eric to grow up with, a big brother looking out for her when she was too shy to speak up for herself. I watched other children with siblings and ached for what Lindsie had lost. Her home had become quiet and lonely. Never thought I'd hear myself saying it, but I even missed the squabbles between Eric and Lindsie. Brothers and sisters can fight all day long and still love each other with an everlasting love. Lindsie was too little to realize the whole of her loss, but I grieved for us both.

Healing

I didn't make a conscious decision to heal. The intensity of my grief gradually lessened enough to where I was developing a routine without Eric; all the while yearning for him, missing him. Knowing without a doubt that Eric was in Heaven gave me assurance that it was okay to begin living again; that it was okay to be okay and he would tell me if he could.

Life will never return to what it was. I knew that losing Eric would change me and the change would be good or bad; I'd either turn bitter and the change would be destructive or I could let this journey with Eric enrich my life. I chose the latter. I wanted to honor Eric and let his life leave me stronger. Once I realized what anger did to my relationship with God, it wasn't as difficult to recognize, and thus, resist. God is a gentleman and He won't intrude where He isn't welcome. At first, I drew in His comfort with nearly every breath, and gradually over time, I found that little by little, my unceasing need for comfort eased.

Longevity of Grief

I grieved for four years. It wasn't a crippling state of grief, like in the beginning. The healing had been a slow steady progression; things that had caused intense pain early on, eventually had less of an impact on me. I think the two most important pieces to healing after a death are faith and time. It's difficult to be patient when you're hurting, and once again, I had to let God lead me through the valley. I also tried to avoid things that might trigger grief. However, there were days when I didn't want to avoid the sadness, and that was okay, I wanted to live in my memories awhile, where Eric was.

Even now, I will have a momentary yearning when I see one of Eric's childhood friends or if I go somewhere that was special to Eric and me. An old cartoon or favorite movie or song of Eric's will take me back. Seeing a young mom with her little boy might carry a moment of pining for my sweet boy with red hair and freckles - I can still feel him in my arms, close to my heart. It's okay, though, because I want to remember him, think about him, and in a sense, embrace him again if only in my heart and mind for a breath of time.

Rather than destroying my faith, losing Eric solidified my faith because I saw God's hand in every moment of the journey, His constant faithfulness. He meant it when He said, *"I will never leave you nor forsake you." Joshua 1:5*. He was with me through the darkest nights, the loneliest days and He counted my tears as He wiped them away. He was there when I discovered Eric's taped love letter, through the people He called to spend time with me, hug me, listen to me. He was there when He gave Eric a firsthand tour of Heaven and He was there when Eric told me about Heaven. I believe God wants to do these very same things for everyone; we just have to be willing to open our eyes, our hearts, and our minds and allow Him into every moment. There is no emptiness, tragedy, disappointment, loneliness that God can't fill with healing and wholeness. I truly stand in awe of Him.

Facing Death

Before I lost Eric, I didn't think about death much. Like I said earlier, I hadn't lost any family members or even an intimate friend. I always felt safe and secure as a child; I don't even remember my parents arguing. I was sheltered, and I was an "emotional cripple" for not ever having to persevere through strife of any kind. I couldn't relate compassionately with others who had. I cared, again, I couldn't relate. But with my own passage through death and devastation, I learned that life and love is fragile; it is to be cherished. Say the "I love you's," the "I'm sorry's," and forgive because you never know what tomorrow will bring.

After traveling through Eric's death and my grief, I want to reach out to others who encounter heartbreak. If God allows, I want to offer the tenderness and compassion I so needed in my own time of mourning. Just to be there in hopefully a sensitive way, and offer genuine companionship through the devastation. I've learned that we all grieve differently: some people heal quietly from the inside out while others, like me, heal from the outside in. I've learned that it's so important to respect the differences, while knowing grief runs to the core regardless of what it looks like on the outside.

I've told God many times He could have chosen another way to grow spiritual character in me. However, I trust God, He is the Potter and I am the clay. I have thought about death, "touched" death, loathed death, accepted death upwards, downwards and everywhere in between, and please know I say this humbly, I am comfortable with death – the death of a Believer. If a person knows Jesus Christ as their Savior, there's no fear in death. I truly love what Paul says in *Philippians1:21* *"to die is gain, to live is Christ."*

I received a card from a relative when Eric died; she wrote "Heaven feels a little closer each time a loved one dies." I understand that. As Believers, we are truly passing through on the way to our eternal home. Heaven doesn't seem like a distant place to me anymore. Now, Heaven is in the forefront of my thoughts. Life's trials take on a different perspective when compared to eternity. I now see death as a temporary good-bye knowing that, in time, we'll be together again, in Heaven, where there will be no more good-byes.

Why Sickness and Death?

I don't blame God for Eric's diseased heart and death. I believe that sickness and tragedy came into the world with the fall, when in the Garden of Eden, Eve believed the serpent's lie and ate the forbidden fruit. He had told her that if she ate the fruit, she would be like God and possess the knowledge of good and evil. I believe His perfect plan for his creation was for us to remain obedient and free from sin, we chose to sin. Our sin separated us from a holy God and so He sent His Son, Jesus, to pay the price for our sin on the cross. Because He did, we can have eternal life, if we accept Him into our lives. I believe there's no other way to Heaven because in the Bible, Jesus says, *"I am the Way, the Truth and the Life and no one can come to the Father except through Me." John 14:6.* I believe God uses our sorrow to turn our eyes to Him. The hurts we bear can cause us to look toward the skies saying "there's got to be something more to this life" and there is. It's called Heaven. Our world will end, but Heaven is for eternity.

Acceptance

My grief gradually turned to acceptance and acceptance was the last piece of the puzzle to make me whole again. For so long, just like Lindsie, I wanted to know why Eric was sick and why he had to die. He was my son. After four years I finally realized "why" wouldn't be answered this side of Heaven. Accepting that I won't know why was when my heart rested. That will never mean I am "okay" with Eric's heart disease and death. I most definitely want my son here with me now. Accepting simply means I trust God and His wisdom. I'll be able to know "why" when it's my turn to follow Eric to Heaven, but when I get to Heaven, I don't think "why" will matter anymore.

My Father God's Love

For most of my upbringing I had no comprehension of God's love. Thankfully, I was raised in strong Bible teaching churches. I went through the motions of Sunday morning Sunday School and church. Knowing me, though, my mind wasn't focused on what was being taught or preached. I think I spent most of the church service watching the clock! We went to family Bible camps and I managed to absorb a little more there, but the spiritual high wore off eventually, until the next summer rolled around and we went to camp again. Of course, I managed to digest a few good things here and there... just enough that I knew I was going to Heaven when I died.

God used my love for my own children to help me understand and trust His love for me. My desire to be a mom was God given. My only purpose in having my children was to love them, hoping they'd love me back. Everything I do for them is out of love, each and every day. There is nothing, absolutely nothing, my children can do to destroy my love for them and so it is with God. If I ask them not to do something, I'm being protective, because whatever it is may hurt them. However, they don't always see it at the time. The Bible says we were created in God's image. Parents and children have similar physical traits: hair color, eye color, height, the list goes on. If I relate all of this to my relationship with my Heavenly Father, I see Him differently. I trust Him.

Thirty Years later

It's been over 30 years since Eric died. So much has changed. Eric's dad and I divorced in the early 1990s. I don't blame it on Eric's death, I've always said that if anything would have kept us together, it would have been that common bond.

God abundantly blessed me with my husband, Steve. We've been married over 20 years and we have a son, Brody, who is now in college. Brody has red hair, like his brother, Eric. God is good. We also have our older kids, Jordan and Lindsie. Lindsie is married and has given us two grandbaby girls and they are a taste of Heaven on earth!

Brody was born 11 years after Eric died. When I was pregnant with Brody, I was surprised with some emotions that I encountered. Our two older kids were in their early teens and were excited about their baby brother. It was Eric that I struggled with, I couldn't tell him that I wasn't replacing him and I sorely agonized over that. These feelings came out of nowhere, like grief seems to do sometimes.

The only question I found offensive after Eric's death was if I planned to have another baby. The question was asked often at first; within days of Eric's death. To me, they were asking, "Are you going to replace Eric?" To think that another child would take all of my pain away, was an innocent inaccurate assumption. I reacted graciously each time, but inside it hurt. In essence, replacing Eric with Brody is also saying to Brody, "You weren't really wanted, we are only having you because Eric died." Not so! I couldn't tell Eric and I so needed to! I actually had some tears over it and had to, again, let God help me work through the emotions. As always, God was right there, faithfully.

Brody is a joy for our whole family. He's the bridge that ties us all together. My only sadness in light of Brody and Eric is that Eric isn't here to make our family complete.

Reflections

As I look back over time at the person I was and the person I am, I know my outlook has changed. My naivety about death and life's hardships has vanished. Death is now tangible to me and I realize that I will encounter more heartache in my life. I don't possess a false sense of security that - it always happens to someone else - because it already happened to me. I could blame it on age, but more than that, I think it's a result of my life experiences. I haven't decided if this is a healthy mindset or as Dr. Gay would say, it's "not being pessimistic, it's realistic."

I catch myself getting anxious when my kids are on the road, when they're sick, or when they're hurting. I worry over them and I don't know if I'd worry less if Eric was alive. The healthy side, though, is that I make sure they know I love them.

I am blessed and thankful that God picked me to be Eric's mom. If I had the chance to do it all again, knowing how the story would go, I'd do it all again. The six years were too short, but I have a lifetime of love stored in my heart waiting for when I see him in Heaven! I've imagined our reunion thousands of times!

I think back to the day Eric died and my mom's sweet friend, Betty, who'd come to comfort me. When she held me and gently told me that she no longer grieved for her daughter, that her little girl had become a sweet memory, I couldn't imagine it. That was before God drew me into His arms and carried me through my darkest hour, because now, thoughts of Eric don't bring sadness, they bring a smile to my heart.

Maybe this is why I needed to wait until now to write this story. Because now I can tell someone who is new to this journey, your memories of your beloved child will one day fill your heart with warmth and God will bless you abundantly through your sorrow. Let Him comfort you. Tell Him how you hurt, don't hold back, but then, let Him love you. Let Him count every tear while He wipes them away. Ask Him to hold your precious child in one arm and you in His other arm, I promise you He will.

I will always have a chamber in my heart that only belongs to Eric. I don't have to search for memories of him; memories of him are always with me. The older I get, the less I look for Eric in my past, but rather, I look forward to being with him again in Heaven.

Biography

Laura Lynn Sargent resides in Indianola, Iowa, with husband, Steve. They have three grown children: Jordan, Lindsie and Brody and two granddaughters: Guinevere and Lucy. They actively attend the Indianola Grace E-Free Church. lauralynnsargent.com